funky, freaky FACTS

most people don't know

THE DIAGRAM GROUP

Sterling Publishing Co., Inc.
New York

Published by Sterling Publishing Company, Inc.
387 Park Avenue South, New York, N.Y. 10016
This book is a combination of two books previously
published as *Freaky Facts* © 1996 and *Funky Facts* © 1996. Each is
A Diagram Book first created by Diagram Visual Information Limited
195 Kentish Town Road, London, NW5 8SY, England
© 1997 by Diagram Visual Limited
Distributed in Canada by Sterling Publishing
c/o Canadian Manda Group, One Atlantic Avenue, Suite 105
Toronto, Ontario, Canada M6K 3E7
Distributed in Australia by Capricorn Link (Australia) Pty Ltd.
P.O. Box 6651, Baulkham Hills, Business Centre, NSW 2153,
Australia

Sterling ISBN 0-8069-4288-6

The most snow to fall in one storm in the United States fell at Mt. Shasta Ski Bowl in California, in February 1959. The storm lasted for seven days, and 189 inches (4.8m) of snow was recorded – enough to bury a small house.

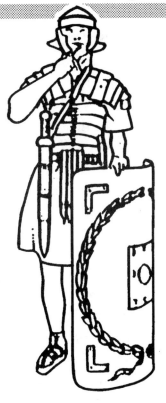

Tasty toothpaste

The first recorded use of toothpaste was about a thousand years ago by a Roman called Scibonius Largus. It was a mixture of honey, salt, and ground glass. Ancient Spaniards dipped their toothbrushes in human urine.

The first robots

The word "robot" comes from the Czech word "robota," which means "forced work." It was used in a play by Karel Capek, called *Rossum's Universal Robots*, which was performed in London in 1923. The first robots appeared in stories as mechanical men which obeyed orders without question. Today, robots are machines which are programmed to carry out certain types of work automatically.

The purity of gold is measured in carats. The top rate of purity is 24 carats, but this is too soft for most jewelry. A common rate is 18 carats – which is three-quarters pure.

Dressed crabs

Spider crabs like dressing up in disguise so much they let other creatures build homes on their backs. These crabs are quite common, but they are difficult to see because they look so much like the seabed.

Losing weight

If you stand on the scales at the Equator, you will weigh less than at the North Pole. This is because the Equator is farther from Earth's center, and the pull of gravity is less.

A queen termite spends her life in the nest, laying eggs. She is fed by worker termites a hundred times smaller than she is. The queen lays as many as 1,000 eggs a day. When she stops producing eggs, she is starved to death.

Walking tall

Did you know that you are taller in the morning than at night? This is because you have soft pads (called disks) between the bones of your spine. They expand slightly overnight, making you taller.

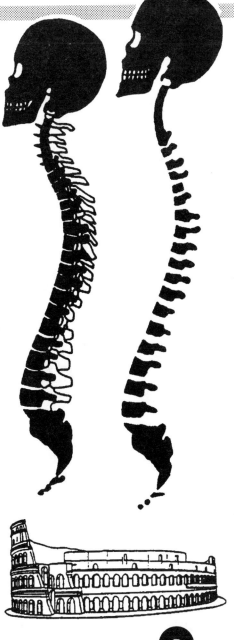

Life and death

The Colosseum in ancient Rome was an arena where people could watch gladiators fight. When gladiators fought each other, the loser died, but the winner was allowed to live.

5

The highest temperature ever officially recorded in the United States was in well-named Death Valley, California, in July 1913. There, about 175 feet (53.3m) below sea level, the thermometer reached 134°F (56.7°C).

Supercharged

Nerve impulses carry messages from your body to your brain at speeds of up to 180 mph (289.6km) – the top speed of a fast car.

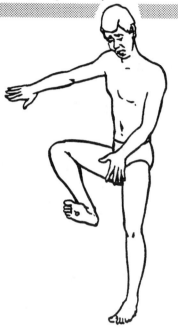

Male mother

A male sea horse has a special pouch on its stomach. The female sea horse lays her eggs in it. The eggs are fertilized and develop in the pouch until they are big enough to be born. Then the male goes into labor and gives birth, pushing the babies out into the sea.

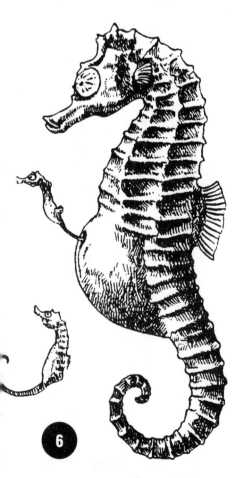

The snake that poisons the most people each year is the king cobra, which lives in India. It has even been known to kill elephants by driving its fangs into the soft tip of the animal's trunk.

Smallest state

Vatican City in Italy is the world's smallest state – less than one-quarter square mile (.6 sq km). Only about 1,000 people live there. It prints its own stamps and money.

The first teddy bears

In 1902, President Theodore "Teddy" Roosevelt, on a hunting trip, refused to shoot a bear cub. The story was printed in the *Washington Post* with a cartoon. A storekeeper cashed in on the story by making toy bears which he called "Teddy's bears."

The Grand Canyon in Arizona is 280 miles (450.6km) long, 1 mile (1.6km) deep, and up to 18 miles (28.9km) across. It was carved out by the Colorado River and took about 10,000,000 million years to get to its present size.

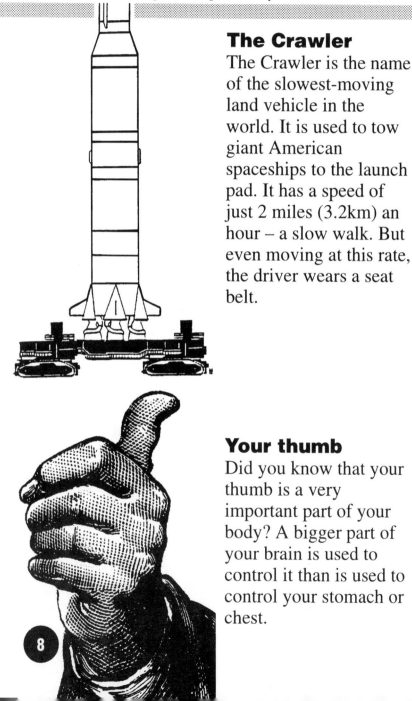

The Crawler

The Crawler is the name of the slowest-moving land vehicle in the world. It is used to tow giant American spaceships to the launch pad. It has a speed of just 2 miles (3.2km) an hour – a slow walk. But even moving at this rate, the driver wears a seat belt.

Your thumb

Did you know that your thumb is a very important part of your body? A bigger part of your brain is used to control it than is used to control your stomach or chest.

The first car had a steam engine and was driven by a Frenchman, Nicholas Cugnot, in 1769. On his first outing he had the world's first car accident, and a year later he was jailed as the first dangerous driver.

Amazing acorns
This is the actual size of an acorn. It can grow into a tree 120 feet (36.5m) high.

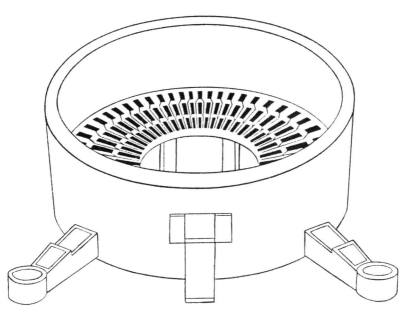

Towers of silence
If you belonged to the ancient religion called Zoroastrianism, you would know about its strange way of dealing with its dead. The Zoroastrians, who live in northern India and Iran, put their dead on platforms, known as Towers of Silence. These round towers are built on high ground so that the bodies, open to the air, can be eaten by vultures.

The most expensive hurricane in the United States was Hurricane Andrew, which hit the Gulf Coast in August 1992. It is reckoned to have caused more than $20 billion worth of damage in South Florida.

Bomb blast

Some people think the dinosaurs died out because of a meteor. This stone – 6 miles (9.6 km) wide – from space hit Earth 65 million years ago.

Fight to the death

Many years ago, two gentlemen settled their arguments with sword fights, or duels, and often died. Duels are now banned everywhere except in Uruguay – as long as the duelists are blood donors.

A sow and her six piglets were sentenced to death for eating a child in France in 1547. The sow was killed, but the piglets were allowed to live because of their youth and the bad example set by their mother.

With a kiss

Kissing has not always meant love. The ancient Romans kissed someone on the mouth or eyes as a greeting. And for centuries, kissing a hand, foot, or the ground a person walked on was a sign of respect.

Mouthful

Some of the dinosaurs that ate other dinosaurs had huge back legs but very small front ones. What they used their front legs for is a puzzle. The legs were too short for pushing food into the dinosaurs' mouths.

The largest reptile in the sea is the Pacific leatherback turtle. It grows up to 7 feet (2.1m) long and weighs nearly 1,000 lb (453.6kg) – more than the weight of five large men.

How many Chinese?

China has more people than any other country – 1,158,230,000 at the last count. That is about one-fifth of all the people in the world. About 14 million babies are born every year – enough to fill a major city the size of New York.

Missing brother

The Marx brothers were a comedy team of real brothers who made many popular films in the 1930s. Three or four of them appeared in the films, but there was a fifth. They were Chico (real name Leonard), Harpo (Arthur), Groucho (Julius), Zeppo (Herbert), and Gummo (Milton), who never acted in a film.

Your skin helps to keep you cool by sweating salty water. On an average day, you sweat about half a pint (.2l), but on a very hot day you can lose as much as 6 pints (2.8l) of sweat.

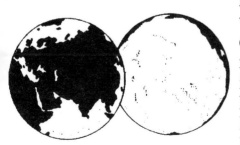

Bird bath

Some birds have a bath, carefully washing and cleaning their feathers. Ducks dip down into the water. Other birds stand in a shallow pool of water or have a shower in the rain. Some birds don't get wet at all. They cover themselves with dust and shake it through their feathers, probably to get rid of lice.

Planet Ocean

Earth is not really the right name for our world. It should be called Ocean because nearly three-quarters of it is covered by water. It has been called the Blue Planet because it looks blue when seen from outer space.

13

The Trans-Alaska pipeline carries oil from the largest oil field in the United States 800 miles (1,287km) from Prudhoe Bay to the port of Valdez. The oil has to be warmed to keep it from freezing in the pipes.

Horse play

In prehistoric times, there was a breed of horses called eohippus. They were only about the size of a cat.

First fries

Potatoes were first grown for food in Peru and Bolivia, South America, more than 1,800 years ago. The Spaniards brought them to Europe in the sixteenth century as an ornamental plant.
A few years later, they were grown for food and soon became popular. There are more than 150 varieties.

The oldest known living thing in the world is a bristlecone pine tree. Growing high up in the White Mountains in California, one tree is reckoned to be 4,600 years old and could live for another 600 years.

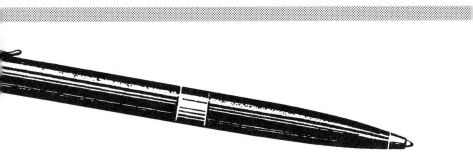

First ballpoint

The ballpoint pen was invented more than 60 years ago by a Hungarian journalist, Laszlo Bíró, who lived in Argentina. He began making the pens in the 1950s. Now millions are sold every day.

Hop it!

Australia's red kangaroos can travel 42 feet (12.8m) in one huge leap. Using their powerful hind legs and holding their small front paws against their chests, they can hop at speeds of up to 40 mph (64.3km/ph) over short distances. They hold up their tails for balance.

A hole in the Arizona desert is almost 1 mile (1.6km) across and over 500 feet (152m) deep. It was made by a huge meteorite, weighing up to 2 million tons (1.8 million metric tons), which hit Earth 20,000 years ago.

Not so extinct?

Some scientists believe that some types of dinosaurs are still alive today. They developed from the early creatures into the birds we now know.

Printing money

Monopoly™ is a popular board game which involves buying and selling houses and hotels. In 1975, twice as much Monopoly™ money as real money was printed in the United States.

The saguaro is the world's biggest cactus. It grows up to 60 feet (18.3m) high in Arizona and Mexico and can hold up to 4 tons (3.6 metric tons) of water. It shrinks in the dry season and fills out again after rain.

Wacky weights

An average woman weighs about the same as 134 rats. A six-year-old child weighs roughly the same as the air in a small bedroom that is 9 x 9 x 8 feet (2.7 x 2.7 x 2.4m).

How many Strads?

Thousands of violins have labels saying they were made by the famous Italian maker, Antonio Stradivari. But most of them are copies – some very bad copies. Stradivari lived to be 93 and was making violins up to the last year of his life. It is thought he made more than 1,100 violins, violas, and cellos – about 600 survive.

There are more than 15,000 different types of flies in the United States, but little is known about many of them. One type, the downlooker fly, stands head down on tree trunks. No one knows what it feeds on.

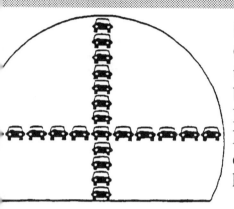

Huge tunnel

One of the largest tunnels in the world burrows under Yerba Buena Island in San Francisco. It is about 11 cars wide and 12 cars high.

Moon flight

The Moon is about a quarter the size of Earth. Flying once around the Moon is about the same as flying from New York to London and back again. One trip around Earth equals four journeys around the Moon.

Have you ever noticed that you breathe more quickly after you have eaten a big meal? This is because you need more energy to digest the food in your stomach, and breathing more quickly helps supply it.

Self-defense

About 200 years ago, an English scientist, Edward Jenner, discovered that giving someone the mild illness cowpox protected them from the serious one called smallpox.

Lobster lines

At the end of each summer, spiny lobsters leave their homes among the rocks and coral beds. They move to another part of the ocean to avoid the great sea storms. They line up in columns of about 70 lobsters. Then they march off at about 18 feet (5.5m) a minute. They walk across the ocean bed all day and night until they find a safer spot to live.

When water freezes into ice, it gets bigger. It also gets lighter and floats on water. If ice did not float, all the seas in the world would have turned to solid ice and nothing would be able to live on Earth.

Swordplay

Kendo is a traditional Japanese martial art based on the skills of the Samurai sword fighters. Today's combatants challenge each other with hollow bamboo poles.

King gone

Richard I, known as Richard the Lion Heart, was king of England for nine years. He spent only six months in England, spending the rest of the time fighting the French and going on crusades to the Holy Land.

A dog can hear a range of sounds – from quiet to loud – two and a half times greater than that heard by humans. A human can make a range of sounds nearly twice as great.

Green giants

Trees are the tallest of all living things. A Californian redwood grows up to 366 feet (111.5m) tall – as high as 63 men.

Not so short 'n' curly

If the bends of the Mississippi were straightened out, the river would be longer than the distance from New York to London. Most maps make the Mississippi look shorter than its 3,710-mile (5,970.5km) length.

In 1946, an earthquake under the Pacific Ocean caused a huge tidal wave. It travelled more than 2,000 miles (3,218 km) at a speed of nearly 500 mph (804.6km/ph). When it reached Hawaii, the waves were higher than a three-story house.

Demon dragons

Do not confuse a dragon with a wyvern. Dragons have animal bodies. Wyverns have birds' feet and snakes' bodies.

High-speed sneeze

Did you know that when you sneeze, air and tiny particles of mucus are blown out of your nose at a speed of 100 mph (160.9km/ph)?

No brakes

Some of the world's largest oil tankers, such as the Japanese *Seawise Giant*, weigh up to 645 tons (585 metric tons) when fully loaded. They are so heavy that when the captain orders the ship to stop, it takes up to 4 miles (6.4km) to come to a standstill.

The world's largest seed looks like a giant coconut and can weigh up to 40 lb (18kg). It comes from the nut palms which grow only on the Seychelles Islands. Some nuts fall into the sea and float for thousands of miles.

Drawing with puff

An airbrush has no bristles, and it is not a brush. It is a tube the size of a ballpoint pen. Air blowing through it forces a fine spray of paint from the nozzle.

Long and tall

The French supertanker *Bellamya* is 1,320 feet (402.3m) long. That is 62 feet 4 inches (18.9m) longer than the Empire State Building in New York, without its mast.

The Sahara, the biggest desert in the world, is almost as large as the United States. Until about 4,000 years ago it was covered with grass and was the home of buffalo, elephants, lions, and antelopes.

Deadly weapon

A bolas spider sets to work making a weapon to kill its prey as soon as night falls. First, it spins a single thread and crawls to the middle of it. Then it carefully makes another thread on which it hangs a ball of spider silk. When the spider swings the thread, the weight of the ball helps to wind the thread around the prey so it cannot escape.

There are about 1,500 different blends of tea. The Chinese and Japanese have drunk tea for thousands of years. The leaves were first taken to Europe about 400 years ago.

Three in one

A mythical creature, the griffin, had a lion's body, the wings of a bird, and the head of an eagle.

Mysterious explosion

On June 30, 1908, something from outer space hit Earth in a remote part of northern Siberia. No one really knows what it was – only that it was a huge fireball. It was so powerful that it melted metal objects and burned herds of reindeer. The blast from it uprooted trees and blew people to the ground.

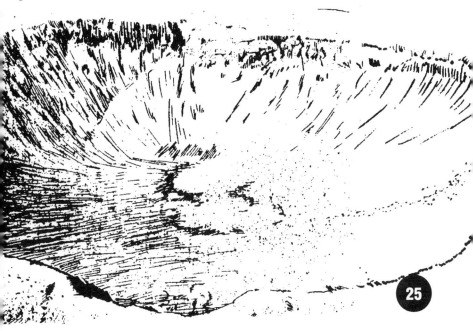

About three-quarters of all the fresh water in the world is frozen in the Arctic and Antarctic ice caps. If they melted, the sea levels would rise by 200 feet (60.9m) and New York, London, and Paris would be under water.

Ballet terms

Ballet, from the French word *bal* meaning dance, developed from spectacles of music and dance performed in Italian and French courts. Until 1681 professionals were all male and wore masks. In the eighteenth century, French ballet was adopted by other countries, so the French terms stuck and are still used today.

1 *Arabesque*
2 *Attitude*
3 *Fouette*
4 *Pas de deux*
5 *Pirouette*

Heaven made

The Hindu god Brahma is often shown with four faces and four arms, representing aspects of the Hindu faith.

The world's first oil well was drilled in Pennsylvania in 1859 by a retired railroad guard called Edwin Drake. Since then, about one-third of all the known oil in the world has been used up.

Underwater whistling

Whales communicate with each other underwater by making whistling, clicking, and moaning sounds. These strange noises, which may be very loud, can be picked up by other whales hundreds of miles away. Male and female whales also leap out of the water and kiss each other. Dolphins too, make sounds, including groans, barks, and squeals. With these noises, whales and dolphins "talk" to each other in languages of their own.

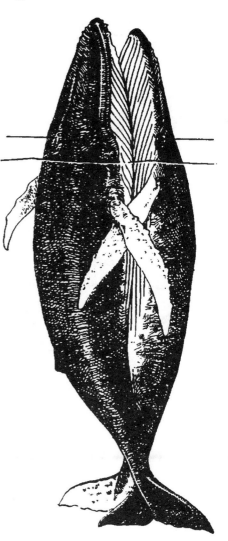

Someone living in a Western country walks about 50,000 miles (80,450km) in a lifetime. Shoes on the right foot usually wear out faster than shoes on the left foot. Why this is, no one knows.

Powerful poison

The poison-arrow frog, which lives in Colombia, is the world's most poisonous creature. One frog has enough poison to kill about 2,200 people.

Building without rooms

Three thousand years ago, the peoples of the Middle East built huge brick temples for their gods. The buildings were solid and in layers, but over the years they have worn away and now look like pyramids.

When the first American telegraph systems were set up, the poles holding up the wires were often pushed over. The herds of wild bison used these poles as rubbing and scratching posts.

Raindrops

For every drop of rain that falls on Cairo in Egypt, there are 23 times more drops falling in London in Britain. In Guinea, on the west coast of Africa, the capital of Conakry has on average more rain each year than any other capital city in the world. The rainfall is 170 times heavier than in Cairo and 7 times heavier than in London. The least rain falls on the Atacama Desert in Chile. There was no rain at all for 400 years and now the record is still nil.

Conakry   **London**

Cairo

Fishermen in Papua New Guinea use spiders' webs as fishing nets. Tropical orb spiders spin webs up to 8 feet (2.4m) across between trees. The fishermen scoop up the web on a loop of stick and catch fish up to 1 lb (453gm) in weight.

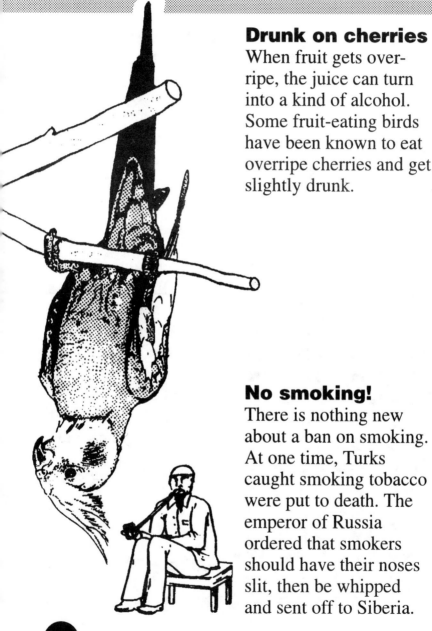

Drunk on cherries

When fruit gets over-ripe, the juice can turn into a kind of alcohol. Some fruit-eating birds have been known to eat overripe cherries and get slightly drunk.

No smoking!

There is nothing new about a ban on smoking. At one time, Turks caught smoking tobacco were put to death. The emperor of Russia ordered that smokers should have their noses slit, then be whipped and sent off to Siberia.

On National Fly-Catching Day in Tokyo, Japan, in 1933, the official count of flies killed was over 117,000,000. Even without a big swat, flies have short lives – females about 29 days, males about 17 days.

Fiery fortunes

The ancient Greeks believed they could tell someone's fortune by staring into the flames of a fire. Some thought the future could be seen in the ashes of a fire that burned a personal possession.

Jumping joeys

Many young animals have names that are different from their parents'. A baby kangaroo is called a joey.

Bison are so big and heavy, they can fight off wolves and are not frightened by them. Native Americans wore clothes made of wolf skins when hunting bison because they could get close without scaring the animals away.

Racing past

The marathon race is named after a flat area in Greece where the ancient Persians and Greeks fought a battle. A messenger raced from the battlefield of Marathon 25 miles (40.2km) to Athens with the news of the Greek victory.

The Great Pyramid

The pyramids of Egypt are the only survivors of what the ancient Greeks called the Seven Wonders of the World. They are still wonders. The oldest, the Great Pyramid, was built as a tomb for the pharaoh Khufu, who died over 4,500 years ago. It contains more than two million blocks of stone. Some weigh 15 tons (13.6 metric tons) – as much as four small cars.

There are more than 3,000 cubic miles (12,500 cubic km) of water in Earth's atmosphere. It is reckoned that if it all fell as rain at the same time, the whole world would be covered with 1 inch (2.5cm) of water.

Tall tales
A bear-like creature, called a megathere, which lived in prehistoric times, was 20 feet (6.09m) high – over three times as tall as an average man.

Golden sheets
Gold is so soft that a lump the size of a matchbox can be flattened out into a sheet big enough to cover a tennis court.

Bread was used as a plate in the Middle Ages. Thick slices of bread, called trenchers, were loaded with meats and other foods for a feast. After the feast, the fatty, soggy trenchers were given to the poor.

Tall stories

The Great Pyramid of Khufu at Giza in Egypt is 175 feet 11 inches (53.6m) taller than the Statue of Liberty in New York, which is 305 feet (93m). The Eiffel Tower in Paris is taller than both of them at 1,052 feet 4 inches (320.7m).

When you dive into water, your heartbeat slows down. This is one of your body's survival tricks. It slows down the effect of the lack of oxygen on your body and helps you to hold your breath longer.

Fooling your foes

Many flies are eaten by other creatures, such as spiders and birds. The lantern fly of Southeast Asia confuses its enemies because it has markings on its rear end that look like a head. Which way is this one walking? Answer: to the left.

Star names

Many actors choose star-like names for themselves. Marilyn Monroe, the famous film star, was born Norma Jean Mortenson (later Baker). She adopted the more memorable name when she began acting in films in 1948.

Squirrel monkeys sometimes leap high out of the trees where they live to snatch flying insects from the air. They may reach a height of more than 60 feet (18.3m) above the treetops.

Name of a dog

A tax collector, called Louis Dobermann, lived in Germany about 120 years ago. He was not welcome when he came to collect money. To protect him, he bred large fierce dogs. They became known as Doberman pinschers and are still used as guard dogs today.

Poles apart

About 600 million years ago, all the world's land was joined together. It slowly split up into today's continents.

Smallest fish

The Marshall Islands goby is the smallest-known fish in the world. Just over one-half inch (1.3cm) long, one would fit on your thumbnail.

Some people grow huge fruits and vegetables. The largest recorded cabbage weighed 114 lb (51.7kg), the largest tomato weighed over 4 lb (1.8kg), and the largest pumpkin weighed 377 lb (171kg).

Walking arch

The Marble Arch in London, Britain, was built outside Buckingham Palace. Because it was too narrow for the royal coach to go through, it was moved more than 100 years ago to its present site near Hyde Park and Oxford Street.

Bugs alive

If you lived 100 million years ago, you may have met an arthropleura. This insect, 6 feet (1.8m) long, lived on forest floors.

A hero shrew has the strongest backbone of any animal in proportion to its size. Its backbone protects it from being crushed when it burrows in the ground. It is said a person can stand on a shrew without harming it.

Full up

At least 12 Greyhound buses would be needed to carry the 500 passengers and crew of just one Boeing 747 jumbo jet.

KO'd by a kangaroo

Rival male kangaroos fight each other with punch-like strokes. When a kangaroo escaped from a Japanese circus, it knocked out three men but was stopped by two policemen with judo skills.

Special spirals

About 100 million years ago, the female dinosaur Protoceratops would lay 12 or more eggs in a sandy hollow nest. She would place them carefully in a spiral with all the narrow ends of the eggs pointing inward.

Chameleons, which are a type of lizard, get their name from two Greek words meaning "ground lion." This is a strange name because all chameleons, except one rare kind, live in trees.

Sleepwalker

The famous French racing driver, Alain Prost, sometimes walks in his sleep. Once he woke up to find himself on a roof!

On track for victory

A Civil War gun was mounted on a railroad car so that it could be moved quickly around the country.

The first escalator in Britain was put in Harrods department store in 1898. An attendant waited at the top and handed a glass of brandy to any customer who was upset by the ride.

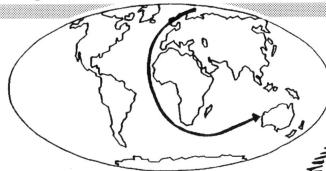

Terrific tern

An arctic tern was found in Freemantle, Western Australia. It had flown halfway around the world – 12,000 miles (19,311km) – from a bird sanctuary on the White Sea coast in Russia.

Barber's striped pole

Men used to go to a barber's shop for a haircut. Each shop had a red-and-white striped pole outside. This was because barbers used to "bleed" people. They cut a person's arm and let it bleed. This was thought to cure some illnesses. Barbers wrapped the used bandages around a pole and left it outside as a sign that they would bleed people.

Stapelia flowers smell like rotting meat, and the leaves look like the skin of a dead animal. This attracts flies that feed on decaying flesh. The hungry flies then pollinate the flowers.

Banned for drinking lemonade

In 1898, a professional boxer fought an amateur boxer in a match in Copenhagen. After the match, the amateur boxer accepted a glass of lemonade from the professional. The amateur was then banned from amateur boxing for having made "material gain" from a fight.

A fire has been burning in Australia for about 2,000 years. It started when a seam of coal in New South Wales was set on fire, perhaps by lightning. The fire is now 500 feet (152.4km) below the ground.

Bigger than a car

Saltwater crocodiles in Northern Australia grow up to 20 feet long (6.1m) – that is longer than a car.

Sharing your bed

Did you know that every night you share your bed with lots of other creatures? Dust mites are so small you can't see them, but there are billions in every house. About a million live in a single bed, munching away on flakes of human skin that rub off all the time. Bedbugs are much bigger, and you know when they are with you. They bite and suck blood.

The Statue of Liberty in New York Harbor was built by a Frenchman, Gustave Eiffel – famous for the Eiffel Tower in Paris. Finished in 1886, the statue was a gift from the French people to the Americans.

Smallest bird

This is the actual size of Helena's hummingbird from Cuba – the smallest bird in the world.

Tribolite eyes

Tribolites were the first animals to have eyes. Some of them had as many as 20,000 lenses in each eye. Human beings have only one. Tribolites lived in the sea millions of years ago and looked a little like wood lice. They became extinct about 230 million years ago, but you can see their fossil remains in many museums around the world.

Each American eats an average of 40 pints (18.8l) of ice cream every year. That is about five times more than the average Briton. The world's largest ice cream was a sundae made in Iowa. It weighed more than 2 tons (1.8 metric tons).

Hard workers

Hummingbirds are very busy birds.
If you worked at the same rate as a hummingbird, you would have to drink almost your own weight in water every hour just to keep cool. And you would have to eat almost twice your weight in food to get enough energy.

Bumps on the head

More than a hundred years ago, a popular way of finding out a person's character was by "reading" the bumps on his head. The shape of his skull and its uneven surface were believed to show all a person's abilities, attitudes, personality, and even if he was likely to be a poet, a drunkard, or a criminal.

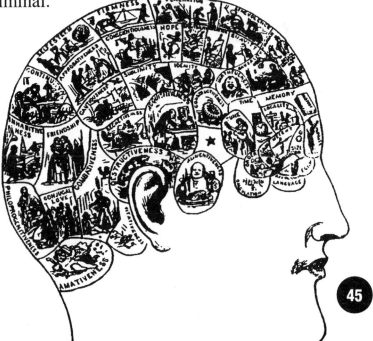

The world's slowest animal is a three-toed sloth. On the ground, it moves at a speed of about 6 feet (1.8m) a minute. It is a little faster in the trees, where it sleeps for 18 hours a day.

Jumping jacks

The gravity of some planets is much less than Earth's gravity. Using the force you need to jump 3 feet (.9m) on Earth, you would leap 9 feet (2.7m) on Mercury.

Inner secrets

Over 3,000 years ago, people tried to learn about their futures by "reading" animal intestines. The head of the giant Humbaba (an ancient Assyrian divination figure) was sculpted to look as though it were made of intestines.

When the first railroads were built in Europe, more than 150 years ago, experts thought that human beings could not travel faster than 20 mph (32.1km/ph). The theory was that at speeds over that, their bodies would explode.

Lucky mothers
Horses have one baby at a time, but pigs give birth to an average of nine babies at a time.

What a stinker!
In 1970, an international competition was abandoned because it was thought to be too dangerous for anyone but the Swedes. The competitors had to eat rotten herrings.

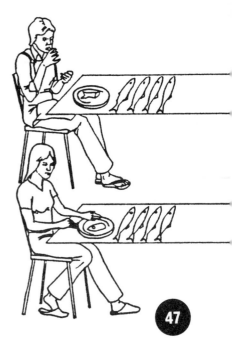

You can draw a line nearly 15 miles (24.1km) long with one ordinary pencil. But the lead in a pencil is not made of lead. It is a mixture of clay and a black mineral called graphite.

Tunnels in trees

Some weaver birds build very unusual nests of reeds in trees. A long entrance tunnel leads to the main part of the nest. This protects the eggs and chicks from hungry predators.

One-piece suit

Ancient Romans wore a garment called a toga. It was a large half circle of woolen cloth which they wrapped around themselves in a special way.

The fastest fish in the sea is the sailfish. It has been timed at just over 68 mph (109.4km/ph) – a good speed for a family car.

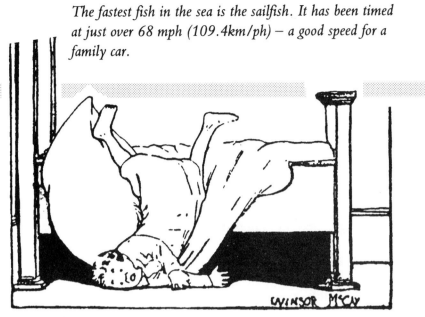

Future dreams

Some people believe that if you dream of climbing up a ladder or stairs, you will be successful. Dreaming of going downstairs means your future will be full of failures and disappointments.

The whistling thorn tree gets its name from the strange music it makes. Some of the balls on the tree have holes made by ants. When the wind blows across the holes, the tree "whistles."

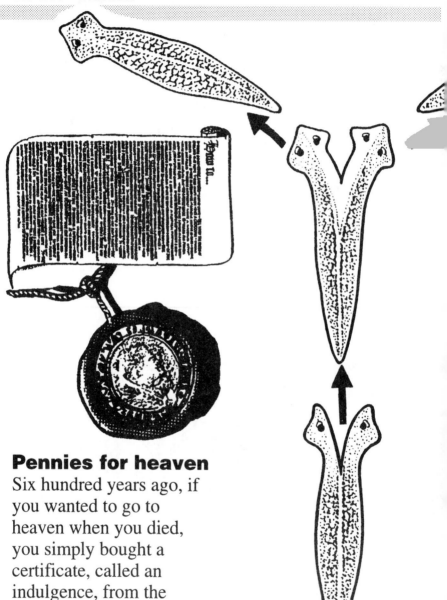

Pennies for heaven

Six hundred years ago, if you wanted to go to heaven when you died, you simply bought a certificate, called an indulgence, from the Catholic Church in Rome.

A cheetah is the fastest animal in the world. It has a top speed of 80 mph (128.7km/ph) but only over a short distance. After about 500 yards (457m), it gets hot and breathless and has to lie down for a rest.

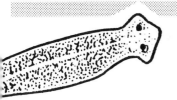

Splitting up

Flatworms don't have to go to the trouble of having babies. After mating, they just split into two new worms. Each one is then both a father and mother.

What a spectacle!

Bifocal glasses, which have special lenses for reading and for seeing distant objects, were invented by the eighteenth-century American statesman Benjamin Franklin.

Pitcher plants feed on insects and even scorpions and lizards. Attracted by sweet nectar, the insects fall into the plant's round, hollow leaves and drown in a pool of liquid at the bottom.

Good dad

A king penguin chick takes 60 days to hatch out of its egg. During this time, the male penguin stands on the Antarctic ice, cradling the egg on its feet and keeping it warm under a flap of soft feathers.

Harder than diamond

Diamond is the hardest known natural substance in the world. It can scratch every other material. The only thing that will scratch a diamond is called borazon. It is made up of boron and nitrogen.

Hundreds and even thousands of prairie dogs live in one huge underground burrow, or "town." Each family has its own part. A sentry at each entrance to the burrow warns of approaching danger.

Fiery breath

A 200-year-old cannon was made in the shape of a sitting tiger.

Kitchen concert

By holding two spoons in one hand, you can clack them to play a tune.

Squirting cucumbers spread their seeds by firing them out of their fruits. The fruits split open and the seeds shoot out at a speed of more than 60 mph (96.5km/ph) and land up to 26 feet (7.9m) away from the plant.

Spider giant

The giant spider crab has a claw span of 12 feet 1 inch (3.7m). Here it is measured against a 17-foot-long (5.2m) canoe.

Lucky aces?

If you have your fortune told with cards, hope that you are dealt the ace of clubs, which means wealth, health, love, and happiness. The ace of spades can mean death.

In winter, reindeer scrape away the thick layer of snow to find green lichen, or "moss," underneath it. Reindeer need more than 20 lb (9kg) of this food every day to stay alive.

Anything goes

Birds will build their nests out of almost anything. Some use their own saliva, while others collect mud, sheep's wool, spiders' webs, feathers, moss, or pebbles. A crested flycatcher uses old snakeskins.

Zombies

Sleepwalkers cannot hear sounds, taste, or smell anything. They only remember what they have done as if they have dreamed about it.

There are more than 8,000 different types of ants in the world. Most of them live in huge colonies in hot, tropical countries. One colony might have as many as 200,000 ants in it but only one egg-laying queen.

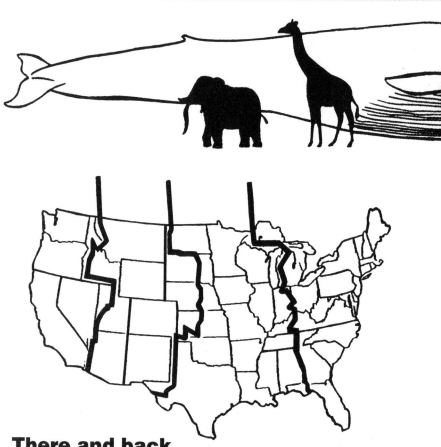

There and back

America is divided into different time zones. From east to west, each zone is one hour behind. If you leave for school at 9:15 A.M. and walk east to west for 15 minutes across a time zone boundary, you would arrive at 8:30 A.M. – 45 minutes before you set off! The same walk home would take 1 hour and 15 minutes!

Nearly 16,000 men died in the first attempt to build the Panama Canal. After nine years, the canal was abandoned, mainly because swarms of mosquitoes gave the workers malaria and yellow fever.

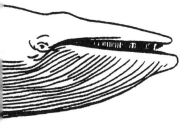

What a whopper!
The largest animal on Earth is the blue whale. Females are bigger than males and weigh about 110 tons (99.7 metric tons). On dry land, the heaviest animal is a male elephant, and a male giraffe is the tallest.

Giant waves
The highest waves ever recorded were in an Alaskan bay. Some were more than 1,740 feet (530.3m) tall – higher than the Empire State Building in New York.

Hyenas hunt at night in packs of about 30. They can run down large animals, which they attack with their sharp teeth. Their usual call is a long howl, but when excited they make a cackling noise.

Pole arms

Pole arms were sharp metal blades and spikes attached to the ends of long poles. Foot soldiers used them before the invention of guns. Here are some fierce examples.

Plankton – a tiny plant that lives in seawater – produces flashes of light. If there is enough of one type of plankton, the light can be bright enough for you to read a book.

Big bones

This man is standing beside the fossilized leg bone, a femur, of a dinosaur. No one knew that the dinosaurs existed until about 150 years ago. When these bones were first found, people thought they were the bones of giant men.

Man against car

From a standing start, a man could beat a modern racing car for about 30 feet (9.1m).

A giant anteater swallows thousands of ants or termites for one meal. It tears open the insects' nest with its long claws, pushes in its tongue – nearly 2 feet (.6m) long – and picks up hundreds of insects.

Ancient temple

The Parthenon, a ruined marble temple stands high on a hill in Athens, Greece. It was the temple of Athena Parthenos, Athena the maiden. The Turks occupied Athens in the 1400s and used the Parthenon as a gunpowder store. It blew up in 1687 and wrecked the temple.

Unique you

No two people have exactly the same fingerprints. This means your fingerprints are different from the fingerprints of all the 5,000 million other people in the world.

Ivy and other climbing plants cling onto walls and trees using tiny roots growing on their stems. The plants only use the trees for support and do not harm them.

Handwalking

Skunks ward off attackers by turning their backs, standing on their front legs, and spraying the enemy with a really foul-smelling liquid.

Whirling weapon

About a hundred years ago in India, Sikhs used a "frisbee" type of weapon. They twirled a razor-sharp metal quoit on one finger and hurled it at the enemy.

Bushbabies hunt for food at night. They have such good hearing that when they sleep during the day, they fold up their ears to cover their ear holes. This stops the noises of the forest from keeping them awake.

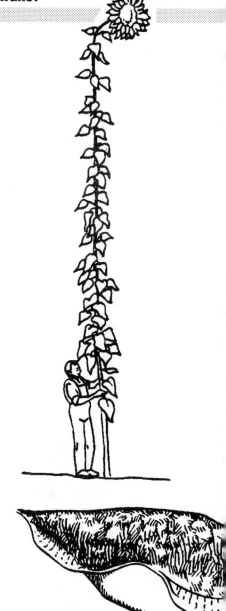

Skyscraper

One of the tallest sunflowers ever measured was 23 feet 6 inches (7.2m) high.

Great grabbers!

Alexander the Great, who lived about 2,300 years ago, ordered all his soldiers to shave their heads and faces. This prevented an enemy from grabbing a soldier by the hair to cut his head off.

Deadly kiss

Cuttlefish, a type of octopus, mate and then both die before their eggs hatch.

Velcro is made of nylon. One strip is covered with tiny hooks; the other has tiny loops. When the two strips are pressed together, the hooks catch onto the loops, and the two strips stick together.

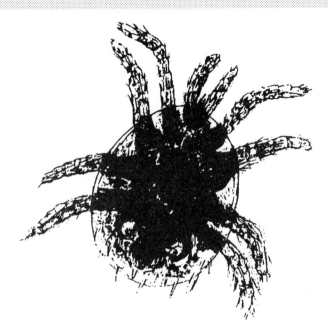

Bee's knees

The creature above has been magnified 100 times. It is really only 1 mm long. It lives on a bee's knees – the bee on the left is shown at its actual size.

Moles keep underground larders of living worms. When a mole finds worms in its tunnel, it eats as many as it can. It then bites the leftovers on their backs to stop them from sliding away.

Skybaby

One of the smallest fully flying planes, the Stits Skybaby, has a wingspan of just 7 feet 2 inches (2.2m). It is shown here against a Boeing 747 jet engine.

Toothless terror

The dunkleosteus lived over 300 million years ago. Even without teeth, this 30-foot (9.1m) fish was a threat to all sea creatures.

When a housefly has finished its meal, it flies off and vomits its food. Then it eats it again. The dirty spots you see on windows are the fly's vomit. It often carries germs that can spread diseases.

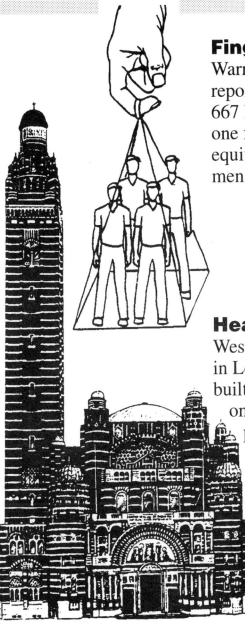

Finger power

Warren L. Travis is reported to have lifted 667 lb (302.5kg) with one finger – the equivalent of lifting four men.

Heaven and hell

Westminster Cathedral in London, Britain, was built on land that was once the site of a prison and a fairground. A former prison, Alcatraz in San Francisco Bay, is now a tourist attraction.

A hippopotamus has huge teeth, but it only eats plants. A female hippo uses her teeth to fight off crocodiles who try to attack her calf. A male hippo uses his teeth to fight other males.

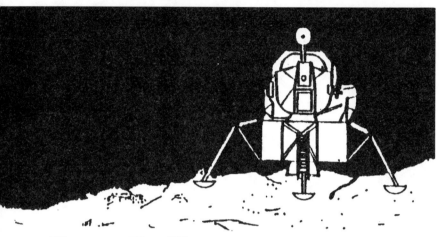

Man on the Moon

Since the first landing by Neil Armstrong on July 20, 1969, 17 other men have walked on the Moon. So far, no woman has had the chance for a stroll.

Tiny tots

This is the actual size of a pygmy shrew. It is 3 inches (7.6cm) from its nose to the end of its tail.

Plants have roots to hold them in the ground and to absorb water and food from the soil. The roots of wheat plants produce slime. This helps the root to slide through the soil as it grows downwards.

Spinning around

Cyclones bring stormy weather. The air in a cyclone spins around and towards its center. Cyclones in the northern half of the world move in a counterclockwise direction. In the southern half, they move in a clockwise direction. This is caused by Earth's spinning on its axis.

Be warned

The Etruscans, who lived long ago in Italy, believed Tin, the god of thunder, sent them warnings to mend their ways. After two warnings, they would be struck by a thunderbolt.

Insects make buzzing noises by beating their wings very fast. The faster they beat their wings, the higher the sound. A mosquito makes a high-pitched whine by flapping its wings about 600 times a second.

100 goals

Native Americans used to play a ball game like baseball. It had up to 600 players, and they were often badly hurt or even killed. The game lasted until 100 goals had been scored.

Legging it

Some creepy-crawlies have lots of legs.
1 Caterpillars usually have 8.
2 "Centipede" means 100 feet, but some centipedes have 354 legs.
3 "Millipede" means 1,000 feet, but the largest recorded number of feet on a millipede is 710.

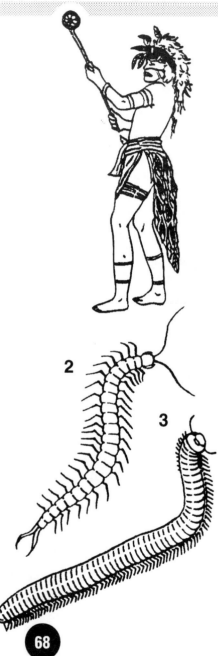

The best and most expensive wool for clothes doesn't come from sheep but from goats. Cashmere is made from Kashmir goats which live in northern India and Tibet. Mohair is made with the wool of Angora goats.

Meteor attack

Over 75 million meteors bombard Earth every day. Most are the size of a pinhead (**a**), and some the size of a grape (**b**). Nearly all of them burn up in Earth's atmosphere.

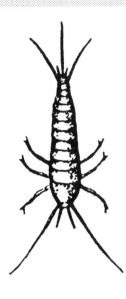

Wrong name

A silverfish is not made of silver and is not a fish. It is a tiny insect that lives in houses, eating anything with paste or glue on it.

Half full

Over half of our bodies are water. Men have slightly more water than women.

A large American possum plays dead when it is attacked. It lies still with its mouth open and eyes staring. If the enemy goes away, it takes a quick look around and comes back to life.

Weighty matters

A bucket of sand on the Moon would weigh about a sixth of what it would weigh on Earth. This is because Earth's gravity is six times stronger than the Moon's.

Not a tapestry

The Bayeux Tapestry is a 230-foot (70m) strip of linen. Its pictures tell the story of the Norman invasion of Britain in 1066. A real tapestry has pictures woven into the fabric. The Bayeux Tapestry is not a real tapestry. It is a piece of embroidery – linen embroidered with wool.

Birch trees produce tiny grains of yellow pollen. One spike may have over five million grains on it. Blown by the wind, the grains land on other birch trees. They pollinate the flowers so the tree can produce seeds.

Faster than a horse

Jesse Owens was a great American athlete who competed in the long jump and in hurdles and who played basketball. He once beat a horse in a 100-yard (91.4m) race.

Mighty midget

This is the actual size of a pistol. It has two barrels and two bullets. If you missed the first time, you got a second chance.

Mojave squirrels dig tunnels up to 20 feet (6.1m) long and 3 feet (.9m) deep in the desert. Away from the heat, they sleep for up to five days a week through the dry winters when there is little food.

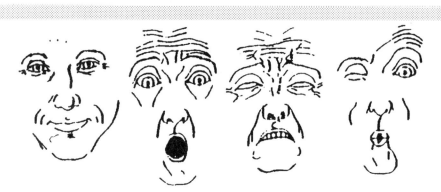

Facing up to it

Our faces show many emotions – surprise, fear, pleasure, and so on. Look in the mirror. How many different expressions can you make?

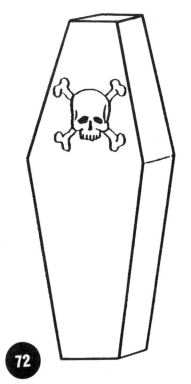

Day of the Dead

The Day of the Dead is a festival held in Mexico each year. It celebrates death, and people have parties around graves, eating chocolates and candy in the shape of skeletons and coffins. In Mexican Indian folklore, the dead return to life on this day.

Potato chips are made by cutting potatoes into very thin slices and frying them in oil. In the chips are tiny pockets of air. When you bite a chip, the crunching sound is the pockets of air exploding.

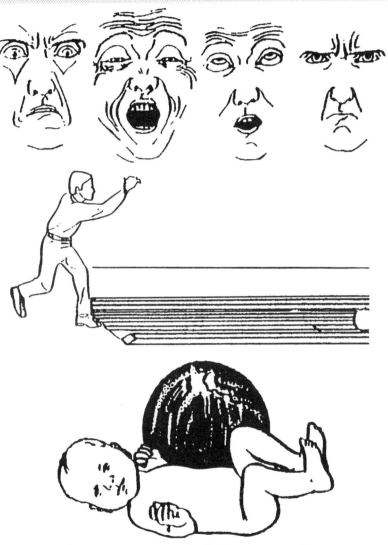

Throwing your weight around

A bowling ball weighs just about the same as an average six-month-old baby – 16 lb (7.3kg).

There are about 1,800 different kinds of fleas in the world. They live on the blood of people, birds, and other animals. Most kinds of fleas prefer one type of animal but will feed on anything if really hungry.

End up

If 26 tiles, each showing one letter of the alphabet, were randomly placed facedown, there would be a 1 in 15,600 chance of turning up the last three to spell "end."

Guardian ants

Bullhorn acacia trees in Central America have a special link with ants. Some kinds of ant live only on these thorny trees and feed on their nectar. In return, the ants drive off insects and larger animals that try to eat the acacias.

Huge chunks of ice break off the ends of glaciers in the Antarctic and float away as icebergs. The biggest iceberg ever recorded was in 1956. It covered about 11,900 square miles (30,702 sq km) — almost as big as Maryland.

Easier to look happy

It takes more than 40 muscles to frown but only 17 to put a smile on your face.

Shrinking water

If you put two spoonfuls of sugar in a glass of water, the water level goes down. This is because the liquid becomes denser and takes up less space.

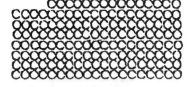

Turned turtle

A female green turtle lays an average of 1,800 eggs in her life. Of these, 1,395 don't hatch, 374 hatch but quickly die, and only 3 live long enough to breed.

Trade rats got their name because they steal shiny things during the night and leave a small rock or twig in their place. There is a story that one trade rat ran off with a lighted candle.

Half-brained

Did you know that your brain has two halves, called hemispheres? The right one controls the left side of your body, and the left one controls the right side of your body.

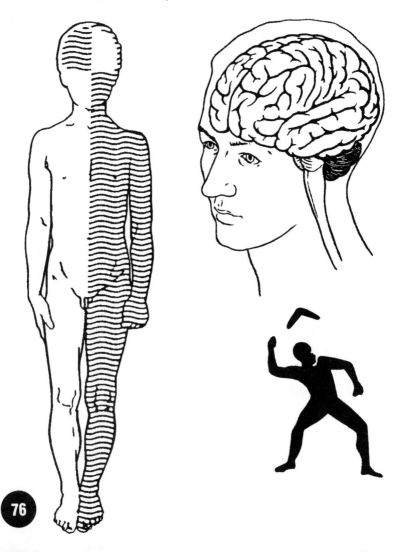

The biggest natural sponge ever found was one called Neptune's cup. It was over 3 feet (.9m) long. More than 4,000 different types of sponge grow in the Mediterranean Sea and around the West Indian coasts.

Razor-teeth fish

Piranhas are terrifying fish. They have rows of razor-sharp teeth and strong jaws. They live in South American rivers and will attack shoals of fish, cattle, and even human beings.

Carved in stone

Wind, rain, and frost wear away rocks and stones into strange shapes, like natural carvings.

Booming boomerangs

Aborigines living in Australia are so good at throwing their wooden boomerangs, they can kill an animal as far away as 500 feet (152.4m) with one.

You have about 62,000 miles (99,200km) of blood vessels in your body. Some are as thick as your forefinger and some as thin as a hair. If they were all stretched out in one line, they would go around the world twice.

Extinct birds that couldn't fly

1 The New Zealand giant moa, the tallest bird, was 11 feet 6 inches (3.5m) tall.

2 The Madagascan elephant bird, the heaviest bird, weighed 970 lb (440kg).

3 The North American "terror crane" was 6 feet 6 inches (1.9m) tall.

4 The largest South American bird was 6 feet 6 inches (1.9m) high.

Seasick seaman

Horatio Lord Nelson was one of Britain's greatest admirals, but he was often seasick for the first few days of a voyage.

A bull moose has the biggest antlers of all deer. They can grow up to 6 feet (1.8m) wide. The antlers are covered with furry skin, called velvet, which a moose rubs off against trees.

Deadly beauty

The Pacific Ocean lionfish eats small fish alive. It is also dangerous to human beings because its spikes have poisonous tips.

3

4

Angel Falls in Venezuela got its name from Jimmy Angel, an American pilot who flew over it in 1936. It is the world's highest waterfall: the river drops 3,212 feet (979m) down the side of Devil Mountain.

Strange serpent

This old musical horn is called a serpent. Made of wood, it has six finger holes. Some serpents were more than 6.5 feet (1.9m) long. They were still played in military bands and in churches until about 100 years ago.

An elephant has the biggest ear flaps of any animal in the world. An African elephant's ears – about 6 feet (1.8m) across – are larger than an Indian elephant's. It flaps them to cool itself down.

The truth about Frankenstein

Frankenstein was not a real person or a monster. In Mary Shelley's book, *Frankenstein*, he was a scientist who created a monster from parts of dead men. So the monster was not Frankenstein but Frankenstein's monster.

The oldest known bird is a royal albatross called "Grandma." She is about 66 years old. Most small birds die before they are a year old. They are killed by other birds, animals, cars, and diseases.

Pedal power

This is the actual size of the world's smallest bike. It was made in Australia in 1974, and its wheels are only 1.25 inches (3.2cm) across.

The only known vampire moth lives in Malaysia. It pushes its long, sharp mouth tube through the skin of buffalo, tapirs, and other mammals and sucks their blood for up to an hour at each feed.

No reverse gear

Sharks are fierce hunters. But, unlike most fish, they have no swim bladders (a kind of buoyancy tank) to keep them afloat. To keep from sinking, they have to be on the move all the time. A shark can swim up and down and turn quickly but cannot swim backwards, like most fish.

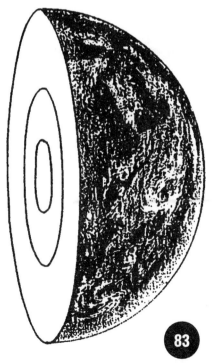

Hot center

If you could cut Earth in half, you would see it has several layers. The nearer each layer is to the center, the hotter it is. At the center, the temperature is 7,600°F (4,205°C) – a hundred times hotter than a warm day.

People were making music over 20,000 years ago. They played flutes made of reindeer antlers and bear bones. They made whistles from hollow bird bones and the toe bones of deer.

Watchful eyes

A honeybee has five eyes. Two of the eyes have a large number of lenses.

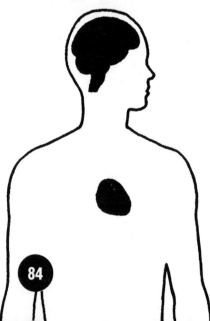

Massive weight

A neutron star is very heavy. Only the size of a pinhead, it weighs as much as a huge ocean liner.

Brainy

Your brain weighs about three times as much as your heart.

The bird with the most feathers in the world is a whistling swan. It has more than 25,000. The bird with the fewest feathers is a ruby-throated hummingbird. It has only 940.

Smallest flower

The artillery flower of India is the smallest known flower in the world. Each bloom is only 0.35 mm (less than a tenth of an inch) across. More than 20 blooms would fit inside this O.

Non-starter

This monocycle was designed by an American over 100 years ago. The rider sits inside the single wheel and pedals it along. It was not a success.

Without green plants, we would all die. Green plants produce all the oxygen that we need to breathe. In sunlight, these plants take in carbon dioxide gas and turn it into oxygen.

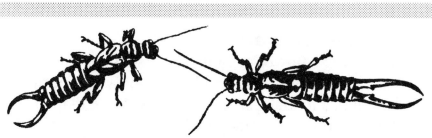

"Ear-ie" creepy-crawlies

Earwigs are small brown insects with pincers on their rear ends. They got their name from an old superstition – people believed they crawled inside a sleeping person's ears and made them sick. Earwigs are, in fact, harmless.

Fishy features

When a human baby, an embryo, first starts to develop inside its mother, it looks quite different from when it is born nine months later. In fact, it does not even look human. At four weeks, it has slits near its neck that look a little like the gills of a fish. At six weeks, it still looks fish-like with a tail as well as arms and legs. After a few months, the gills and tail disappear, and the embryo begins to look human.

When the Kariba Dam on the Zambezi River in Zimbabwe began to fill up with water in 1959, there were hundreds of earthquakes. The weight of the water was forcing rocks to shift underground.

Long haul
It took six powerful engines, three pulling and three pushing, to move the world's largest freight train in West Virginia. The 500 coal trucks stretched for 5 miles (8km).

Hopeful mothers
The sunfish holds the record for producing the most eggs. She can lay up to 300 million at one time.

Fleas live on hedgehogs, making their homes among the prickles. Even smaller creatures – so small you can only see them with a microscope – creep between the scales of the fleas.

The dreams of Dickens

Oliver Twist, Mr. Pickwick, Fagin, and many other characters all came from the dreams of the famous author Charles Dickens.

The nails on your fingers and toes grow very slowly – just over 1 inch (2.5cm) in a year. A man in India grew one thumbnail until it was more than 45 inches (114cm) long.

Sweet partnership

The honey guide bird got its name because it guides honey badgers to where honey is stored in a bees' nest in a tree. The honey guide loves eating honey and even beeswax but cannot break into the nest on its own. Chattering loudly, the bird leads a honey badger to a nest. The badger breaks open the honeycombs, and the bird and the animal share a feast.

Flick 'n' lick

A chameleon's tongue is as long as its body. It shoots it out to catch flies.

Sand dunes are always on the move, burying everything that stands in their way. The wind blows the sand up one side of a dune, and the sand slides down the other, slowing moving forward.

Eggstra special

An ostrich lays the largest egg in the world – it is 6–8 inches (15–20cm) long. That is longer than a man's hand. A hummingbird's egg is under half an inch (1.3cm) long.

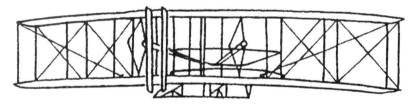

Bicycles to planes

Before making the first airplanes, Orville and Wilbur Wright were bicycle makers. Flyer 1, in which Orville made the first flight, weighed 560 lb (254kg). when empty – 20 times more than a modern racing bicycle.

You can see dark patches on the Moon even without a telescope. Before telescopes were invented, people thought these patches were water and named them "seas." But there is no water on the Moon, and nothing can grow.

Lucky you

You may be lucky or unlucky – it depends on the cat and where you are. A black cat is unlucky in America but lucky in Britain.

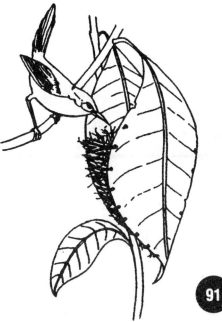

Needlework

A tailor bird gets its name from the way it builds its nest. It sews two leaves together, using its beak for a needle and plant fibers for thread.

A human has a total of 52 teeth in a lifetime. The first 20 are lost by the age of 13 and are eventually replaced by 32 adult teeth.

Double vision

A rabbit's eyes are positioned so that it can see objects in front of it and behind it at the same time.

Hands on

In ice hockey, a goalkeeper's two gloves are very different from each other. One is for the stick hand and the other for the catching hand.

When a honeybee finds a flower with plenty of nectar, it drinks the nectar and then flies back to its hive. There it does a special little "dance" to tell the other bees where to find the nectar.

Pickled brains

Charles Babbage, who lived 200 years ago, is credited with inventing the first computer. When he died, scientists put his brain in a jar of preserving fluid. It is still there today for all to see.

Empty graves

In some parts of the world you can see standing stones, topped with horizontal ones. These were underground tombs, dug over 2,000 years ago. Since then, the earth over them has been worn away, exposing the stones.

Crater Lake in Oregon was formed about 7,000 years ago when Mt. Mazama erupted in a huge explosion and the sides of the mountain fell. The crater which it left gradually filled with water.

Dangerous women

There were four dangerous female creatures in mythology. **1** The Harpy had a woman's head and a bird's body. **2** The mermaid had a woman's body and a fish's tail. **3** The siren had a woman's body and a bird's wings and legs. **4** The sphinx had a woman's head and a lion's body.

Goalie's goal

A goalkeeper once kicked a ball from his own goal area the length of the entire soccer field. It bounced into the opponent's goal!

When you are born, you have more than 800 bones in your body. By the time you are grown, you have only 206 bones. Some of your bones, including some that make up your skull, join together as you grow.

Ant herders

Some ants keep herds of aphids – tiny insects that live on plants – like people keep cows. The ants protect and look after the aphids. They "milk" them by stroking them with their antennae. The aphids then produce drops of clear liquid, which the ants quickly lick up.

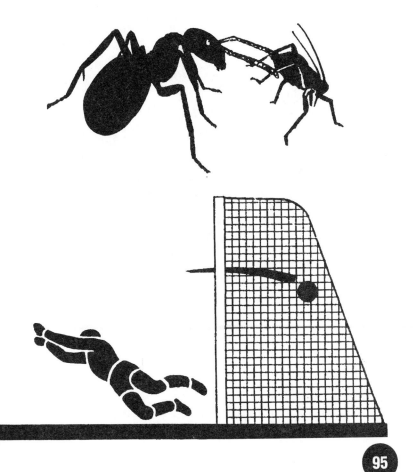

Billions of snowflakes fall on the ground every year, but each one is different. Snowflakes are made of tiny ice crystals which freeze together in the clouds. Most of them have six sides.

Crying wolf
If you had a mental illness called lycanthropy, you would think you were a wolf.

The footprints left by astronauts walking on the Moon will still be there in a million years. There is no wind, rain, or water on the Moon to wash or blow the footprints away.

Pedaling high

An American cyclist, Bryan Allan, pedaled into the sky on a self-propelled glider-bike. It weighed only 70 lb (32kg) – the weight of a ten-year-old child.

Moving stage

The landlord of the Globe Theatre in Britain, where William Shakespeare and his friends acted nearly 400 years ago, raised the rent. The actors took down the building and put it up on another site.

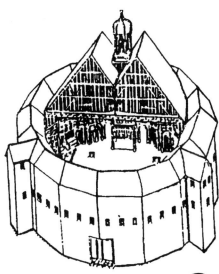

Fulmars protect their nests by spitting an oil at any predator that comes near. The oil is made in the bird's stomach from the food it eats, and it smells terrible.

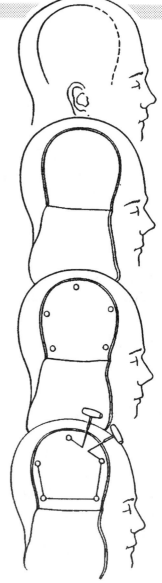

Holes in the head

If something goes wrong inside your head and a surgeon has to operate on part of your brain, she first cuts a flap of skin to reveal your skull. Then she drills five holes in your skull and cuts around the holes with a saw. She lifts off the cut bone to get at your brain. When the operation is over, she reattaches the piece of bone and sews back the flap of skin. Of course, you are unconscious during the operation.

Tiny ant

Some ants are so tiny, they could fit inside this letter o.

The Amazon River is the second largest river in the world. One-fifth of all the world's river water flows out of its mouth into the Atlantic Ocean. Starting as a stream in Peru, it is nearly 4,000 miles (6,437km) long.

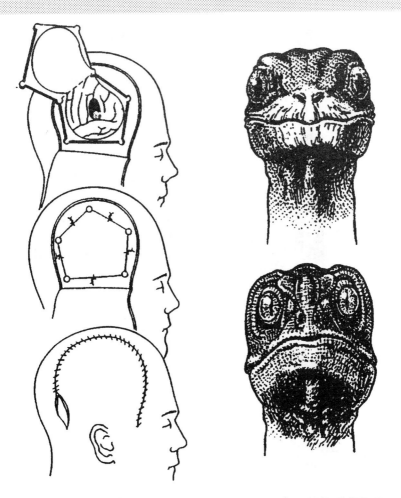

Watch out!

A dinosaur with eyes on the sides of its head, like a horse, could see an enemy coming from the side or even from behind. A dinosaur with eyes on the front of its head could only see forwards. These were the ones that chased and ate other creatures.

Some plants spread their seeds by using animal or bird carriers. When an animal or bird brushes against the plant, the seeds stick to their fur or feathers. The seeds drop or are rubbed off miles away.

Channel tunnel

The first plan for a tunnel between Britain and France was conceived by the French emperor Napoleon Bonaparte nearly 200 years ago. Nothing was done until 1875, when digging began on the French side. This was stopped because British generals feared it could be used by the French to invade England. The present tunnel was completed in 1993 and opened in 1994.

Sheepskin or chamois leather?

Real chamois leathers are made from the skin of "goat antelope" or "chamois." A lot of leather cloths you wash cars with are really made from sheepskin.

The world's longest mountain range is mostly underwater. The Mid-Atlantic Ridge is 9,942 miles (15,997km) long and stretches all the way from the north Atlantic Ocean to the Antarctic.

Money bird

Male quetzal birds have beautiful long tail feathers which were once worn by ancient Mayan chiefs as a symbol of authority. Now the bird is Guatemala's national symbol, and the country's money is named after it.

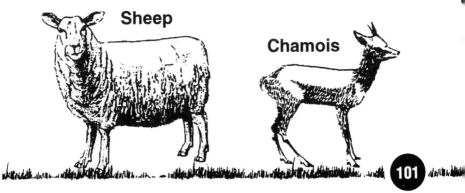

Sheep

Chamois

There are about 250,000 different types of flowers in the world – and that's not counting all the flowers that have been specially grown for their size, color, and scent.

Misplaced

Can you see the fish, a plaice, in this picture? Some fish are able to change the pattern and color of their skins to match the sea floor on which they lie.

Safe on high

American inventor Elisha Otis built the first safety elevator in 1852. Such elevators allowed builders to construct very tall buildings.

Some spiders are big enough to eat birds. They live under logs and in holes in the ground in forests in South America, Africa, and Asia. Their bodies are as big as oranges and their legs as long as pens.

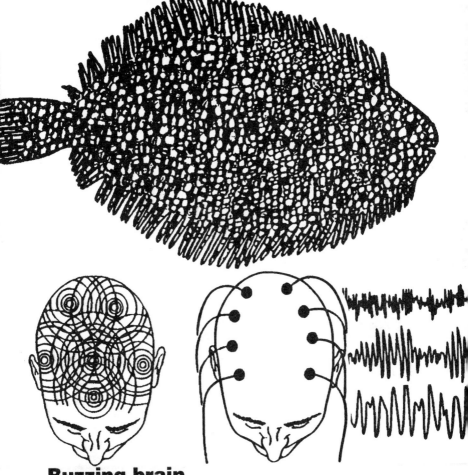

Buzzing brain

Your brain gives off tiny electrical signals. Electrodes attached to your head can pick up these signals and record them on a machine. These "brain waves" show how you react to various things and what condition your brain is in.

The River Ganges is sacred to the Hindus of India. The riverbanks are lined with temples, and steps – called ghats – lead down to the water. Every year thousands of Hindu pilgrims go to bathe in the river.

Helpful hands

A shrimp has nineteen pairs of arms or legs. You have only two pairs. It uses two pairs to find food in the water, one pair as jaws, five pairs to handle the food, five pairs to walk with, five pairs to swim and breed, and the last pair as a tail.

Animal weed killer

Manatees are used in Guyana to keep waterways clear of weeds. A fully grown manatee is 16 feet (4.9m) long and eats 100 lb (45kg) of weeds a day – about the same as 1,500 small bags of potato chips.

Human warble flies lay their eggs on female mosquitoes. When the mosquito lands on a human being to bite him, the warble fly eggs hatch, and the maggots burrow into the person's skin.

Roman frontier

For seven years, starting in AD 122, Roman soldiers worked to build a wall across northern England to keep out raiders from Scotland. It is called Hadrian's Wall, after the emperor who ordered it built. It had a rampart 15 feet (4.6m) high, with a deep ditch on the Scottish side, and forts at intervals. You can still walk along parts of it today.

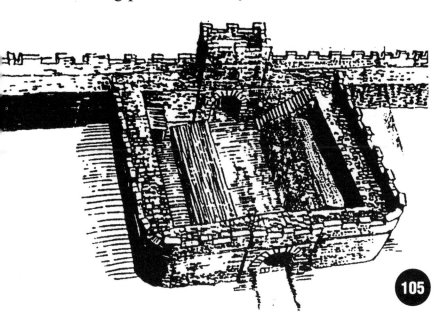

Mt. Etna, on the island of Sicily, is the highest active volcano in Europe. It has erupted 260 times since it was first recorded nearly 3,000 years ago. Liquid rock hums and roars inside the volcano.

Short life

A mouse lives for only two or three years – on average human beings live 25 times longer.

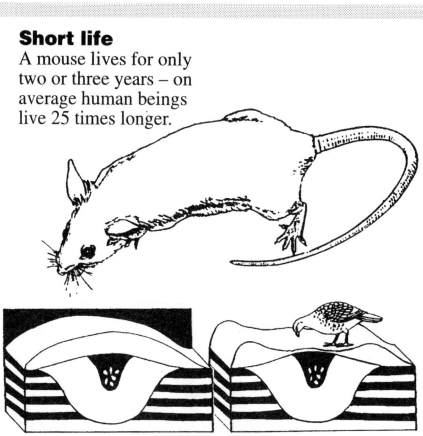

What a pile up!

An Australian bird called a mallee fowl makes the biggest nest in the world. First it scratches up a huge mound of plants. It lays its eggs in a hole in the center and then heaps more plants on top. As the plants rot, they heat up, keeping the eggs warm until they are ready to hatch. The bird opens the nest to cool it down during the day and covers it up at night.

Stegosaurus may have been the stupidest of all the dinosaurs. It had a big, heavy body that weighed up to 2 tons (1.8 metric tons), but its tiny brain weighed only about 2 ounces (56gm) – as much as one chicken's egg.

Young genius

The great composer Wolfgang Amadeus Mozart was writing piano pieces by the time he was five. He was only six years old when his father took him on a concert tour.

Wonder worm

The record length for a South African earthworm is 22 feet (6.7m) – the length of seven garden spades.

Your ears tell you if you are standing up, leaning over, or lying down. Special cells in tubes of liquid in your inner ear send messages about your movements to your brain. They help you to know what you are doing.

Half men

In ancient Greek mythology, there were creatures with a man's head, arms, and chest but with the bodies of animals. A centaur had the body and legs of a horse. A triton had a horse's front legs and a fish's tail.

Leopards store their food in trees, where it is safe from jackals and hyenas. After a leopard makes a kill, it feeds on the meat. Then it drags the remains of the animal up a tree and hangs them from a branch.

Mega spider

This is the actual size of the world's largest spider – the South American bird-eating spider.

Devil's Tower in Wyoming stands 869 feet (264.8m) above the Belle Fouche River. According to a Native American legend, the strange ridges down its sides were made by a giant bear trying to reach the people on the top.

Not a piggy

Tapirs, which live in Central and South America and Malaysia, look a little like pigs. But they do not belong to the pig family. Only about 3 feet (.9m) tall, they are related to horses and rhinos.

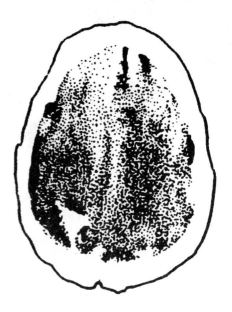

Cat's eye

The special method of using X rays called computerized axial tomography (CAT scan) was invented in 1973. Doctors use it to look at what is going on in a living body.

There are probably over 80 million different types of insects in the world. This is more than all the different types of animals and plants. And each type might include billions of insects.

Boneless fish

Manta rays, like other rays and sharks, have no bones. Their skeletons are made of tough cartilage or gristle.

Female support

The first bra was made by an American, Mary Phelps Jacob, in 1914.

You have about five million hairs on your body. Many of them are so fine, you can hardly see them. They grow at an average rate of up to .5 inch (1.3cm) a month but a little faster when the weather is warm.

Short leg

Colin Jackson won a gold metal for Britain in the Olympic hurdle race in 1988. What few people knew was that he had a pad in his left shoe. This was because his left leg is .5 inch (1.3cm) shorter than his right leg.

Old teeth for new?

The earliest known false teeth were worn by the Etruscans in central Italy about 3,000 years ago.

A housefly walks on the ceiling, clinging on with its six feet. On each foot are tiny tubes which act as suction pads. The tubes also release a sticky substance which helps the housefly walk on smooth surfaces.

Great Wall

The Great Wall of China is the biggest structure in the world. It runs across northern China for 2,162 miles (3,480km), with branches and spurs almost that long. It was built more than 2,000 years ago to keep out raiders from the north.

Loud howler

Howler monkeys live in the tropical forests of South America. They howl at dawn, when two groups meet, and when they are disturbed. Their roars can be heard nearly 2 miles (3.2km) away.

Greenland is the largest island in the world. Most of the land is covered with sheets of ice. The temperature is usually below freezing, and it snows all year round.

Mother tongue
The mother of Joseph Stalin, former leader of Communist Russia, never learned to speak the Russian language.

Getting at it
Some birds drop stones onto other birds' eggs to crack them open. Then they eat them. Gulls drop crabs from a height to break open the shells. A woodpecker finch pushes a sharp stick into cracks in trees to pick out grubs and insects.

The stars you can see on a clear night are part of our galaxy, the Milky Way. It is so big that if you drove a fast car across it, the journey would take about 665,000 million years.

Tuned in

Some scientists think that there are people who can read minds and "see" what others are thinking.

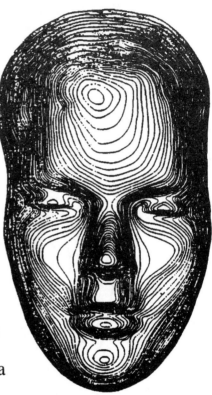

Field landing

A jumbo jet is 195 feet (59.3m) long – well over half the length of a soccer field.

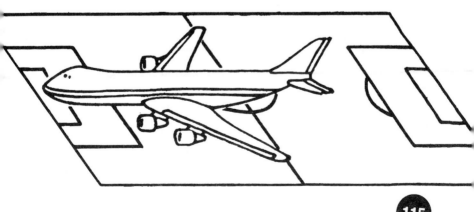

About 10 million free-tailed bats are born each year in Bracken Cave in Texas. The babies hang onto the walls of the cave while their mothers go out to find food. Each mother always manages to find her own baby.

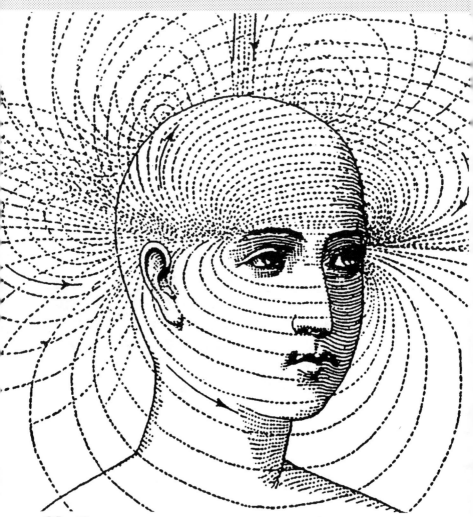

Sixth sense

Human beings have five senses – touch, sight, hearing, taste, and smell. Some people believe we have a sixth sense that alerts us to danger and that gives us glimpses of the future.

One of the world's most poisonous creatures is a type of jellyfish called a sea wasp. It lives in the Pacific Ocean. After being stung by a sea wasp, a swimmer sweats, goes blind, cannot breathe, and dies in a few minutes .

Mother's boy

The gangster Al Capone could not talk to his mother when she visited him in prison. Only English was allowed, and she spoke only Italian.

Pickled!

British admiral Horatio Lord Nelson was wounded at the Battle of Trafalgar against the French in 1805. He died on his ship *Victory*. To stop his body from decomposing on the long journey back to England, it was put into a barrel of brandy.

When Mt. St. Helens, in Washington state, exploded in 1986, 1,300 feet (396m) blasted off the top of the volcano. Hot gas, steam, ash, and rocks shot out, killing millions of birds, animals, and fish.

Winning by a beak

In South Africa, jockeys wearing full racing colors race on ostriches.

Long life

The oldest recorded tortoise was 152 years old – that is twice the average life span of most human beings.

An orangutan, a very large ape, builds a nest in the trees every night. It makes a mattress out of bent branches in the fork of a tree and covers itself with a blanket of leaves, all in about five minutes.

Shocking treatment

Some scientists believe that when a person is hypnotized, an electrical magnetic force is transmitted by the hypnotist.

A roadrunner can reach a speed of 25 mph (40km/ph). Dashing across the deserts of North America, this bird chases snakes until they are too tired to fight back. Then it kills them with its sharp beak.

Bird snatcher

The ancient Greeks believed there were women with birds' bodies called Harpies. They stole food from their victims.

Super snail

This is the actual size of the head of the world's largest snail. It lives in Africa, and it is four times as long as the width of this page.

The Sun is a star that you can see during the day. It is a very hot ball of hydrogen gas. It uses up about 4 million tons (3.6 million metric tons) of gas every second but it has enough to keep going for another 5,000 million years.

Grave error

The painter Vincent van Gogh was named after a brother who had died at birth. All Vincent's life, there was a grave with his name on it.

Big blast

In 1783, a volcano erupted in Iceland. It released a huge cloud of dust and gas which caused the deaths of 10,500 people and floated for months over Europe.

In only a few square miles (sq km) of rain forest there may be 700 kinds of trees, 1,000 different flowering plants, 450 different kinds of birds, 100 different animals, and 100 types of moths and butterflies.

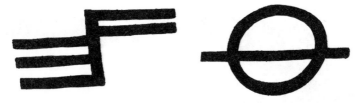

Long walk

Captain Scott and his team of explorers walked 950 miles (1,528km) from the Antarctic coast to the South Pole. On their return, they ran into trouble and all died. If they had succeeded, their journey would have been the same as walking from London to Moscow in temperatures well below zero.

Below the line

Every merchant ship has a line on its side, showing the level it can sink to when safely loaded. It is called the Plimsoll line, after Samuel Plimsoll, a British Member of Parliament, who campaigned against the danger of overloading ships.

Flamingos get their orange-pink color from their food. They eat shrimps and tiny water plants that contain an orange substance called carotene. Without this food, their feathers slowly turn a dull gray.

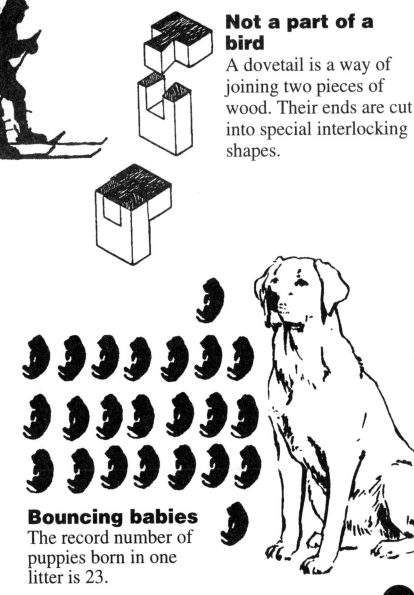

Not a part of a bird

A dovetail is a way of joining two pieces of wood. Their ends are cut into special interlocking shapes.

Bouncing babies

The record number of puppies born in one litter is 23.

A Portuguese man-of-war jellyfish has tentacles up to 65 feet (19.8m) long. They are covered with spines which shoot poison into anything that touches them. The poison kills fish and is very painful to people.

Night sight
Modern soldiers have special telescopes fitted to their rifles so they can see in the dark.

Long flier
Painted lady butterflies fly from North Africa to Iceland.

Glyphs for numbers
Ancient Mayans in Mexico used pictographs to represent numbers.

1	2	3	4	5	10

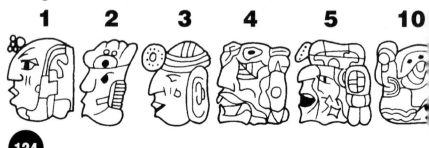

In 1955, red snow fell on the Alps in Europe. The snow was colored by dust which had been carried by winds from the Sahara desert in North Africa, over 1,800 miles (2,895km) away.

Pining away

A pineapple does not grow on a pine tree and is not an apple. It got its name because it looks like a pine cone.

Quick march

You can easily tell a centipede from a millipede – centipedes have four legs on each section of their bodies; millipedes have only two.

Wolves howl to tell each other where they are and to call the pack together at the end of a hunt. Sometimes the whole pack will howl. One starts, and the others join in. They can be heard more than 7 miles (11km) away.

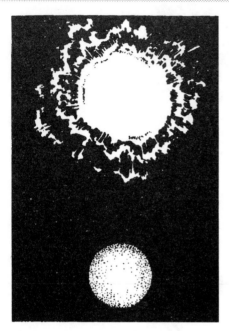

Age of the Earth

In 1654, Archbishop James Ussher of Ireland used the Bible to determine that Earth was created in 4004 BC. We now know that it is at least 4,600 million years old.

Quick families

The record number of baby mice born of one mother at one time is 34.

Adelie penguins spend the winters feeding far out at sea. In September and October, they go back to their nests on the ice and snow in the Antarctic. They can't fly, but they waddle up to 200 miles (322km) across the ice.

Reverse again

When you take a photograph, the image you capture is reversed in three ways. The top is at the bottom, the right is on the left, and the light areas appear dark.

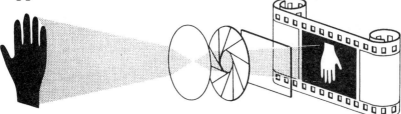

Largest number

Red-billed queleas are thought to be the most numerous birds in the world – there may be more than 10,000 million in Africa.

Six fingers

Anne Boleyn, the mother of Queen Elizabeth I of England, was born with six fingers on her right hand.

Outer space is not empty. There are lots of rocks, dust, pieces of meteorites, and comets. There are also used rockets, old and broken satellites, and even tools dropped by astronauts.

Lucky hand
You get just one combination out of 2.5 million when you are dealt five cards from a 52-card deck.

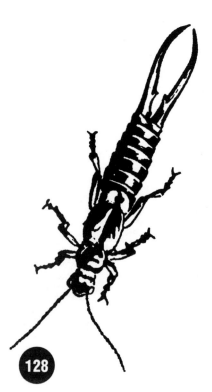

Male or female
You can tell male from female earwigs by the shape of their pincers. A male has curved ones, and a female has straight ones.

Beavers can cut up a log 20 inches (.5m) thick with their sharp teeth in just 15 minutes. They cut down trees to make a dam and then build their home, called a lodge, in the pond which forms behind the dam.

Useful neighbors

Birds called yellow-rumped caciques build their nests next to wasps' nests in South America. Most animals will not disturb a wasps' nest. So the caciques' nests are protected by their stinging neighbors.

Riding on air

The air-filled bicycle tire was invented twice. The first inventor was a Scot, Robert Thomson, but he did not develop it. Another Scot, John Dunlop, began manufacturing his air-filled tire more than 100 years ago.

The world's greatest travellers are Arctic terns. Each year, these birds fly all the way from the Arctic to the Antarctic and back again – a round trip of more than 25,000 miles (40,225km).

Chew on this

George Washington had several sets of false teeth. They were made from elephant tusks, lead, and cow, hippo, and human teeth. It is said he soaked his false teeth in wine each night to make them taste good.

Stinging tale

Scorpions were the first animals in the world to live on land. They have been around for 440 million years.

Tall buildings sway and bridges tremble in gale-force winds. The bridge over the Tacoma Narrows in Washington state shook so much it was called "Galloping Gertie." It eventually fell down in a violent storm.

A smasher!

Birds can be very clever at getting the food they want. A thrush smashes a snail's shell against a stone to get at the flesh inside.

Paris gun

This huge gun was used by the German army to shell the city of Paris at a distance of 74.5 miles (120km) in World War I.

A Canadian porcupine has over 30,000 quills on its body. If it is attacked, it backs into its enemy, pushing in its needle-sharp quills. Then it walks away, leaving a few quills behind.

Rain rattles

The Hopi Indians of the southwestern United States used to try to make it rain in their desert area. They danced around with rattlesnakes in their mouths, pleading with the rain gods to send them showers.

Golden nose

Tycho Brahe, the famous astronomer, had part of his nose cut off in a sword fight. He had a false nose made of gold, silver, and wax. It was painted to look like skin. He wore it for 30 years, until he died in 1601.

Have a banana!

Ancient Greeks, Romans, and Arabs ate bananas. Early explorers took them across the Atlantic to the Caribbean islands.

The world's biggest clamshell is more than 3 feet (.9m) across. Stories that fishermen's feet have been trapped by the clam are not true. Its shell closes so slowly, they have plenty of time to escape.

Ancient insects

Over 280 million years ago, giant insects like dragonflies lived on Earth. This was long before there were dinosaurs. You can see their descendants hovering over ponds and streams.

The wandering albatross has the longest wings in the world. They are up to 12 feet (3.6m) from wing tip to wing tip. This bird flies over 500 miles (804km) a day across the south Indian Ocean, using the air currents.

Slow mummy

It took the ancient Egyptians ten weeks to prepare a dead body and wrap it, before putting it in a coffin.

*Humpback whales catch fish in a net of bubbles. A whale swims
under the fish and squirts out a circle of bubbles from its blowhole.
The fish stay inside the circle, and the whale then swallows them.*

Love apples

Tomatoes were once
called love apples
because people thought
they inspired love. They
were grown for food by
Native Americans long
before Columbus
arrived.

Bird planters

Thick-billed nutcracker birds, native to
Scandinavia, hide stores of nuts to eat during the
winter. Although a bird remembers where it buried
the nuts, it sometimes misses a few. These grow
into trees, helping the forest to spread.

Crows make about 300 different sounds to call to each other and to warn off enemies. Crows live in many parts of the world, and, like people, they have different languages in different countries.

Glittering gold
Gold does not tarnish or corrode but stays bright forever. It is a very soft metal and can be hammered into any shape.

Anting
Some birds use ants to clean them. They sit with their feathers fluffed up and let the ants crawl over them. The ants squirt out an acid which kills the insects living on the birds.

The loneliest people in the world are the 300 or so who live on Tristan da Cunha in the Atlantic. This is the most isolated inhabited island on Earth. Their nearest neighbors are 1,320 miles (2,124km) away.

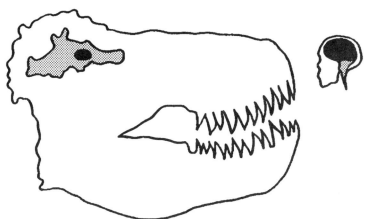

Brainy

Although the brain (the gray area) of the dinosaur Tyrannosaurus was bigger than a human's, the thinking part – the black area – was much smaller.

Bugs alive

This is not a monster but a tiny bug, only 1 mm long. It can live on your body, biting and sucking your blood. It's called a crab louse.

137

Mudskippers use their fins to skip over the mud of mangrove swamps in Southeast Asia. These strange fish can breathe through their skin when out of the water and through their gills when they are in the water.

Leaping lions

Lions are shown on badges, coins, flags, and stamps. There is a special name for each way a lion leaps, stands, sits, or lies.

1 Lion rampant
2 Lion statant guardant
3 Lion rampant guardant
4 Lion passant
5 Lion statant
6 Lion passant guardant
7 Lion sejant
8 Lion sejant rampant
9 Lion couchant
10 Lion salient
11 Lion coward
12 Lion queue fourchée

Thousands of mammoths have been found frozen in the ice in Siberia in Russia. Looking like big wooly elephants with long curved tusks, these animals died between about 25,000 and 40,000 years ago.

So many cells

The back of your eye is called the retina. Although it is quite small, it contains 137 million cells. It has 130 million cells to help you see black and white, and 7 million cells to help you see colors.

This is the actual size of your retina.

Mini molecules

A molecule is a tiny piece of something, so small you can only see one with a powerful microscope. Molecules are so tiny that one spoon of water contains as many molecules as there are spoons of water in the Atlantic.

The male bellbird is one of the loudest birds. Sounding like a clanging bell, it can be heard over half a mile (.8km) away. It sings to attract a mate. When a female comes close, it dances out and sings again.

Typecast

Over 100 years ago, some scientists believed that the shape of your head showed the type of personality you had. Are any of your friends' heads shaped like one of these?

1

2

Future dinosaurs

If the dinosaurs had not become extinct, some scientists think they could have developed to walk upright and look like human beings.

Oil is processed to make fuel for cars. It is also used to make medicines, explosives, pesticides, detergents, glues, polishes, paints, nylon, plastics, and even makeup.

1 Idiot
2 Criminal
3 Poet or thinker
4 Likely to commit crimes
5 Likely to be honest

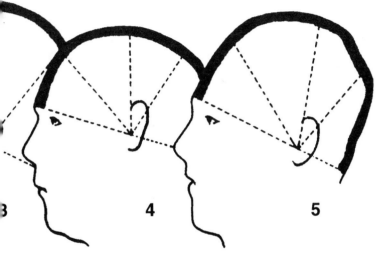

3 4 5

Startling eyes

When this moth has its wings folded, it looks like a piece of old bark. If a bird comes near, it opens its wings and shows two spots that look like eyes. The startled bird is likely to fly off without trying to peck at the moth.

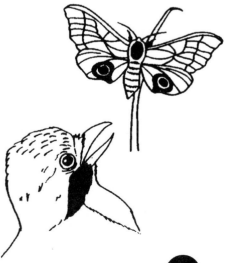

African baobab trees have very fat trunks which they use to store water. The trunks of some old baobabs are hollow and have been made into bus shelters and even homes for people to live in.

Box gogglers

It is estimated that by the time you are 18 years old, you will have watched more than 15,000 murders on television and seen more than 360,000 commercials.
In all, you will have spent 17,000 hours in front of the box.

Royal palace

A great palace was built at Versailles, outside Paris, in the seventeenth century for the French king Louis XIV. It had a Hall of Mirrors 240 feet (73m) long, lit by 3,000 candles. In the gardens were 1,400 fountains. The palace was open to the public, and people could wander through its rooms and even watch royal births.

The oldest known clothes are about 37,000 years old. They were found on the body of a man frozen in the ground in Siberia. Made of animal skins, they were sewn together with strips of leather.

What a corker!

Table tennis was invented by James Gibb over 100 years ago. It was first played with paddles made from cigar-box lids and champagne corks for balls. The game is also called Ping-Pong™.

Walking on water

A South American lizard can walk on water, but not for very long. It has powerful back legs and broad feet with fringed toes that keep it afloat. When scared by a predator, the lizard leaps from the riverbank and dashes across the water for as long as it can. Once it sinks, it can stay underwater for up to two minutes.

Diplodocus was one of the longest dinosaurs to have lived on the Earth. It was about 85 feet (25.9m) long, with a neck about 25 feet (7.6m) long. Although it was so big, it ate only leaves and plants.

Whose side are you on?

The pages of this book each have two sides. Turn over and look at the back of this one. You can make a strip of paper that has only one side. You don't believe it? Take a strip of paper. Twist it once and glue the ends together. Now try to color only one side of the whole strip.

Pedal power

A bicycle, ridden by three men and mounted on canoes, traveled down the River Thames from Oxford to London in Britain faster than an ordinary boat rowed by three men.

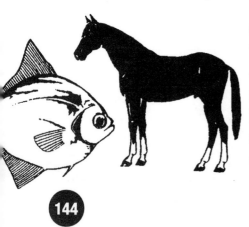

Outnumbered

There are more than 4,000 different types of mammal, including human beings. But there are more than 23,000 different types of fish.

A male Adelie penguin finds a mate by dropping a rock in front of another Adelie penguin. If the bird is female, she bows, and they mate. If it is male, it pecks the other male very hard.

Friendly foe

Gorillas in zoos eat meat. Those in the wild eat only fruit and vegetables.

The biggest eggs were laid by the elephant bird. They were over seven times bigger than an ostrich's egg and weighed about 22 lb (10kg). This extinct bird, which looked like a large emu, lived in Madagascar.

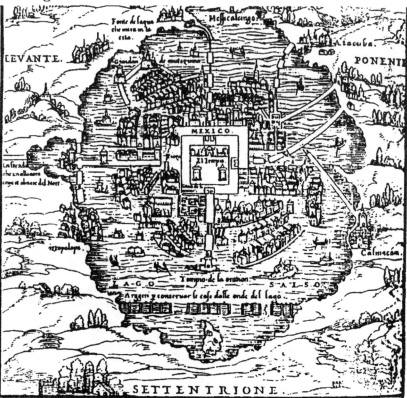

Sinking city

Mexico City is built on an underground reservoir. Each year, the number of people in the city grows, and more water is taken out of the reservoir. As a result, the city is slowly sinking at a rate of about 6–8 inches (15–20cm) a year. This picture shows the city in the middle of a lake at the time when Europeans first explored America.

Geysers appear when water is heated by hot underground rocks in volcanic areas. There are more than 10,000 geysers at Yellowstone Park. Old Faithful geyser spouts 130 feet (39.6m) into the air every 30 to 90 minutes.

Head-bangers

Some dinosaurs fought for food or for mates by charging at each other and banging heads. Called "boneheads," they had thick skulls to protect their brains.

Sowing seeds

This bracket fungus, a type of mushroom, sheds its seeds, called spores, at a rate of 30,000 million a day for six months.

Manta rays are as big as a small plane, with "wings" up to 21 feet (6.4m) across. They flap their wings to swim slowly through the sea. Although they look scary, they are harmless and feed only on tiny sea creatures.

Talking trees

Scientists have discovered that trees may be able to talk to each other using a chemical language. When one tree is attacked by caterpillars which feed on its leaves, it sends out chemical signals to other trees. The trees' leaves make substances that the pests dislike, and this prevents the caterpillars from spreading to the other trees and eating them, too.

The Gulf Stream speeds across the Atlantic Ocean, bringing mild weather to Europe. New York is only 100 miles (160km) north of Lisbon in Portugal, but when it is freezing in New York, it can be quite warm in Lisbon.

Always in touch

Every part of your body is connected by nerves to your brain. The smallest change in temperature or softest touch sends a message to your brain, asking for action.

Head start

Most dinosaurs had very small heads. **1** Torosaurus was an exception and had the largest head of any land animal. **2**

Huge harpy eagles fly low over the rain forests of South America. Speeding through the tree tops, they use their claws to snatch monkeys, sloths, birds, and even porcupines to eat.

Skin tight

The ancient Mexican god of spring, Xipe Topec, wore a coat made of the skin of a sacrificed human.

Bigger billions

An American with a billion dollars has $1,000,000,000. A Briton with a billion pounds has £1,000,000,000,000. The European billion is 1,000 bigger than the American billion.

The first people to live in Australia sailed there about 30,000 years ago. They were the Aborigines, who crossed 40 miles (64km) of open sea from Indonesia and gradually spread all over the country.

On its back

This tiny shrimp, called a brine shrimp, swims along upside down, moving its tiny legs like the oars of a rowing boat.

Lengthy lungs

Did you know that your lungs contain a mesh of very small blood vessels called capillaries? If you laid them out end to end, they would stretch for 1,500 miles (2,414km).

Pelicans have huge bags of skin under their beaks. They use them like nets to catch fish in the water. When their bags are full, the birds drain out the water. Then they toss their heads and swallow the fish whole.

Strong grass

Would you make furniture with grass? Some people do. Bamboo is a type of grass, the largest grass in the world. Its hard, woody stems are so tough they are used to make houses, chairs, tables, beds, flutes, and stakes for garden plants. There are more than 700 kinds of bamboo. Some grow up to 122 feet (37m) tall.

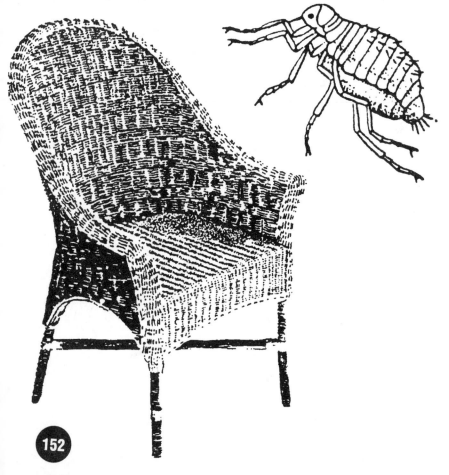

The biggest reef in the world is the Great Barrier Reef off the east coast of Australia. It is over 1,000 miles (1,609km) long. More than 400 different types of coral are busy building and repairing the reef.

Giant pearl
One of the largest pearls, the Pearl of Laotze, was found inside a giant clam. It was 9.5 inches (24cm) long and weighed as much as a three-month-old baby.

Killer fleas
A deadly disease, called the bubonic plague, killed more than a quarter of all the people in Europe in the fourteenth century. The disease was spread from rats to human beings by tiny biting fleas.

Guard dog
In ancient Greek mythology, the gates of the underworld were guarded by a dog with three heads, called Cerberus. It allowed only spirits of the dead to go in and let none out.

Every year gray whales swim from their feeding grounds in the Arctic to the coast of California, where they breed. They return when their calves are two months old – a round trip of about 13,000 miles (20,917km).

Colorful warning

The male anole displays his colorful throat flap to attract a female and warn off other males in the mating season. It is a member of the chameleon family.

Milestones

The current record for running one mile is 3 minutes, 44.39 seconds. It was set by an Algerian, Noureddine Morceli, in 1993. Until 1954, people thought it was impossible for anyone to run a mile (1.6km) in under four minutes. In that year, an English medical student, Roger Bannister, ran it in 3 minutes, 59.4 seconds.

Bald eagles build the world's biggest nests. Each year the eagles use the same nest, adding more branches. A nest can be 9 feet (2.7m) across, 18 feet (5.4m) high, and weigh as much as a large car.

Single parents
Male and female jaguars live apart all the year and only meet during the mating season. The female gives birth to 2–4 young and brings them up on her own.

Old paper
The oldest surviving writing paper dates back to about AD 110 and was made in China.

There are about one trillion (1,000,000,000,000) birds in the world. Over eight billion (8,000,000,000) of these are chickens reared for food. That is enough chickens for everyone in the world to have one and a half chickens each.

Superstition

Alberto Ascari won 20 Grand Prix races. He was so superstitious that he always drove wearing a lucky blue helmet and shirt. In 1955, he tried out a sports car without them and was killed.

Read all about it!

The first newspaper was printed in China about 1,300 years ago. It was called *Tching pao* – "News of the Capital." Another early government newspaper called *Acta Diurna* – "Daily Happenings" – was handed out free in ancient Rome.

The west side of a city is often a better place to live than the east side. In places with a temperate climate, the wind often blows from the west, bringing clean air and carrying smoke and dust eastwards.

Castle on a volcano

Edinburgh Castle in Scotland was built nearly 1,000 years ago on top of an old volcano. But there is no need to worry. The volcano, and another one nearby called Arthur's Seat, became extinct about 300 million years ago.

A green heron catches fish with bait. The bird drops an insect onto the water. Then it stands very still and waits. When a fish swims up to the bait, the heron spears its prey with its beak.

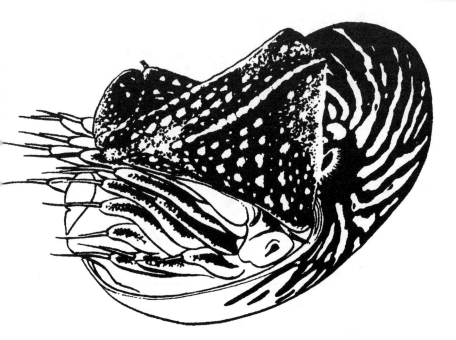

Moving house

A shellfish called a nautilus lives in a compartment in a coiled shell. As it grows, it moves out of the old compartment and builds a bigger one in front of it.

Nearly one-tenth of the world is covered with ice. The biggest ice sheets are in the Antarctic and in Greenland. The Antarctic ice sheet is one and a half times the size of the United States.

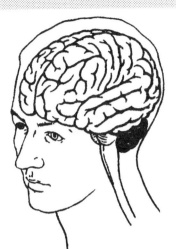

Wacky weights

An adult's brain weighs 3 lb (1.3kg), which is equal to the weight of three soccer balls.

Exploding balls

During World War II, the Germans dropped iron balls full of explosives (mines) into the sea. When a passing ship bumped into the floating ball and touched a point, the bomb exploded.

Niagara Falls will disappear in about 25,000 years. The river is very slowly wearing away the rocks on the edge of the Falls. About 10,000 years ago, the Falls were 7 miles (11.2km) downriver.

Getting around

Over 300 years ago, an English doctor, William Harvey, was the first to discover that your blood moves around your body. The blood in your big toe today may be in your ear tomorrow.

Not a home

Two-story stone houses built in the English Lake District were not for people. They were winter shelters for cattle.

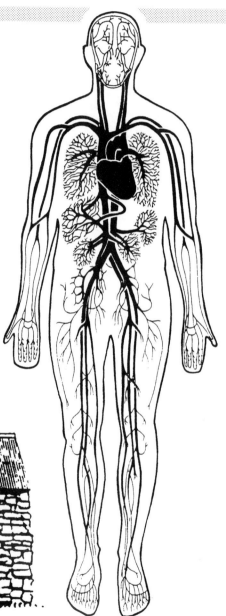

When the first cinema opened in Hong Kong, people had to be paid to go in. The Chinese believed the "moving spirits" on the screen had evil powers. But they soon got over their fears and paid to watch movies.

Blood suckers

Vampire bats really do exist. They live in Central and South America and feed mainly on the blood of cattle. They bite their skin with sharp teeth. A special substance in their saliva stops the blood from clotting while they lap it up.

Nose greeting

Eskimos say hello, goodbye, and kiss by rubbing noses.

Owls have huge eyes for hunting in the dark. Some can see fifty times better than a human being. An owl can't move its eyes to look to one side, but it can turn its whole head around to look backwards.

Good looker

Human beings' eyes face forward. They can see ahead and to each side. Fish, with eyes on the sides of their heads, can see behind them as well as in front.

In a thunderstorm, lightning and thunder happen at the same time. You see the lightning flash first and then hear the thunder because light travels faster than sound.

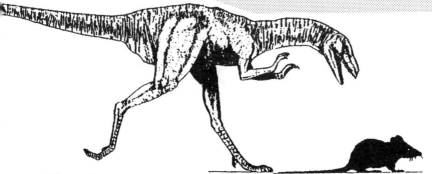

Tiny terror

Not all dinosaurs were huge monsters. This one, which lived about 150 million years ago, was only the size of a cat.

Back to front

No. 10 Downing Street, the official home of the British prime minister, is back to front. The famous front door is really the back entrance to two houses which are now joined into one.

"Mysterious dogs"

Native Americans caught and rode horses first brought to North America by Europeans. The Indians called them "mysterious dogs."

Yellowfin tuna are the fastest fish in the sea. When they see, hear, or smell their fishy food, they can reach a top speed of 45 mph (72km/ph) in a second. If they stop swimming, they sink slowly to the bottom.

Pet monster

The hellbender is a giant salamander, about 30 inches (76cm) long. When kept as a pet, it will eat dog food.

Growth check

A baby grows fastest in the last three months before it is born. If it continued to grow at that rate it would be 18 feet 4 inches (5.6m) tall by 10 years of age.

All the cereals we eat and feed to animals have been developed over hundreds of years from wild grasses. They include wheat, corn, rice, oats, barley, millet, rye, and sorghum.

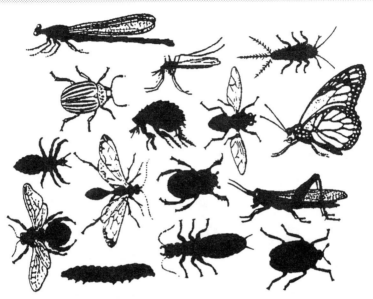

Creepy-crawly
Of all the different species of animal on Earth, nearly half of them are insects – there are over 950,000 different kinds.

Satchmo
Louis Armstrong, the great American jazz musician, learned to play the trumpet while he was in an orphanage in New Orleans.

Trumpeter swans take off from the water like a plane on a runway. To build up enough speed to get into the air, these heavy birds flap their wings and run across the water until they are airborne.

High divers

Professional divers in Acapulco in Mexico dive into water from rocks 118 feet (36m) high – equal to diving from the roof of an 11-story building.

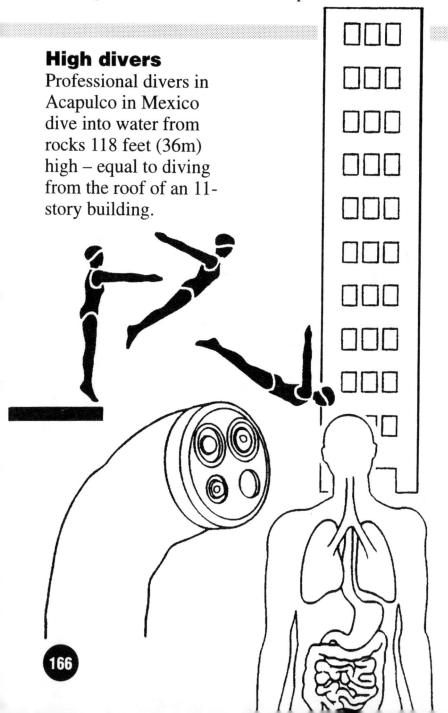

Waves wear away the coasts all the time. At Martha's Vineyard in Massachusetts, the cliffs are being worn away at a rate of about 5 feet (1.5m) a year. The lighthouse there has been moved inland three times.

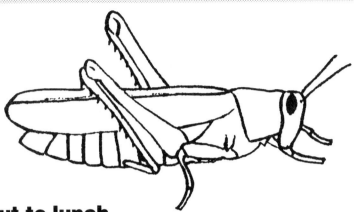

Out to lunch

A swarm of North African locusts can be so big it forms a black cloud which blocks out the Sun. A single swarm may have over 50,000 million locusts in it and cover 400 sq miles (1,036sq km). A swarm feeds at dawn and dusk, eating 3,000 tons (2,721 metric tons) of plants every day.

Inside view

Doctors can now look inside your body without having to cut you open. They insert a very thin fiber-optic tube. At the end of the tube are a light and a tiny camera. The camera sends back pictures so the doctors can see what is wrong with you and if you need surgery.

The tallest clouds are the great towering thunder clouds, called cumulonimbus. They can be twice the height of Mount Everest, the tallest mountain in the world, and hold 500,000 tons (453,500 metric tons) of water.

From out of the sky

There have been many reports of animals and fish falling out of the sky. No one knows how they get up there, although some people think they are swept up by strong winds. Here are some examples.

1 Bergen, Norway, 1578. Yellow mice fell into the sea and then swam ashore.

2 Singapore, 1861. After an earthquake, fish fell on the streets and bucketfuls were picked up.

3 Tennessee, USA, 1877. Thousands of snakes dropped out of the sky during a rain storm.

4 Birmingham, Britain, 1954. Hundreds of frogs fell on people's heads and hopped around in the streets.

5 Maryland, USA, 1969. Hundreds of dead ducks dropped down onto the streets.

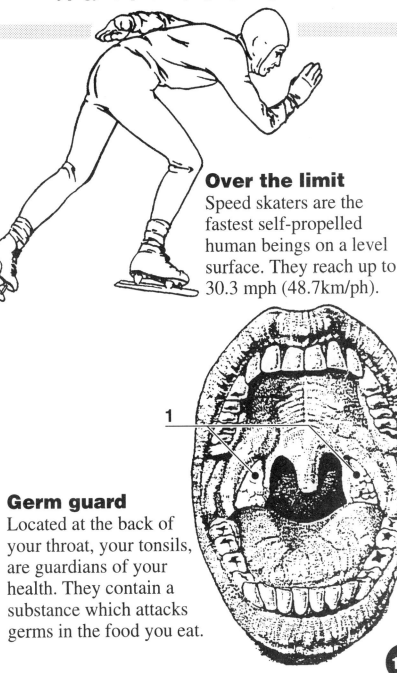

Frigate birds are the fastest of all the sea birds, with a top speed of 93 mph (150km/ph) . They steal food from other birds while flying and catch flying fish, squid, and jellyfish floating on the water.

Over the limit

Speed skaters are the fastest self-propelled human beings on a level surface. They reach up to 30.3 mph (48.7km/ph).

1

Germ guard

Located at the back of your throat, your tonsils, are guardians of your health. They contain a substance which attacks germs in the food you eat.

The famous composer Beethoven began to go deaf when he was only 26. He was completely deaf when his Ninth Symphony was first performed in 1824. He helped the conductor keep time but could not hear the applause.

Head styles

Dinosaurs' head shapes reflected the ways they lived.

1 A large hollow nose to make loud barks.

2 Powerful jaws to chew meat.

3 A thick skull to protect the brain when banging heads in a fight.

4 Horns to fight and parrot beak to bite.

5 A pincer mouth for crushing eggs.

6 A swanlike beak for snapping at prey.

Saltwater crocodiles are the largest reptiles in the world. They grow up to 20 feet (6m) long. When a crocodile catches a big animal in its jaws, it turns over and over in the water to drown it before eating it.

Inside story

There are worms that live in animal and even human intestines. Some are tiny, but a tapeworm can grow up to 30 feet (9.1m) long.

Feather talk

Native Americans who lived on the plains wore feathers in their hair as a mark of victory over the enemy. The position of a feather and the paint on it carried messages, like these:

1 I was the third to wound the enemy in battle.
2 I killed three.
3 I cut his throat and scalped him.
4 I was wounded in battle.

Kiwis hunt for food at night using their noses. Most birds have noses at the base of their beaks, but kiwis' noses are at the tip. In the dark, they sniff out worms and insects to eat.

Getting the hump

There are two types of camel. A dromedary has one hump with a back like a D on its side. A Bactrian camel has two humps with a back like a B on its side.

Meatless monster

Adolf Hitler, the leader of the Germans during the 1930s and World War II, is said to have never eaten meat.

Sign of the times

The Chinese used a shadow clock to tell the time more than 4,500 years ago.

HITLER

Flying fish beat their tail fins from side to side and leap out of the sea at over 35 mph (56km/ph). They spread their side fins and glide through the air to escape from fish that are chasing them.

Fastest ever
Astronauts returning from the Moon in command module Apollo 10 in 1969 reached a speed of 24,791 mph (39,888km/ph).

Fossil clues
Fossilized evidence of dinosaurs includes:
1 footprint **2** droppings **3** print of skin **4** eggs

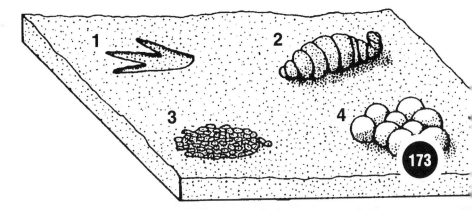

There were no sparrows or starlings in North America until about a hundred years ago when a New Yorker imported the birds. He wanted the United States to have all the birds named in Shakespeare's plays.

Moon station?

These castles on legs were built in Britain 50 years ago. Standing at the mouth of the River Thames, they guarded London from attack from the sea.

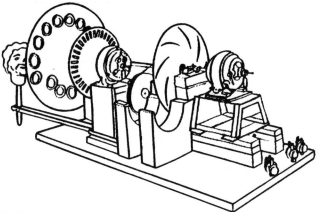

Junk box

The first television was made by John Logie Baird, a Scottish engineer, in 1924. He used cardboard, scrap wood, needles, and string for some of the parts.

You see a rainbow when the sun, shining on drops of water, is broken up into seven main colors. On the ground, you only see half a rainbow. In a plane, you see the whole circle of a rainbow.

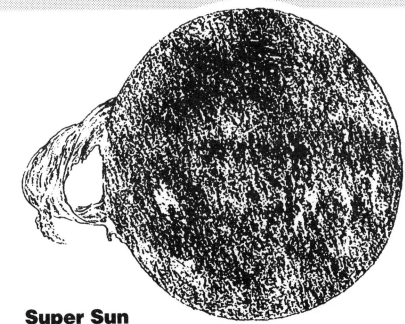

Super Sun

Did you know that the Sun is 93 million miles (150 million km) from Earth? If you drove a car at 55 mph (88.5km), you would take 193 years to reach it. It is a ball of gas with a surface temperature of 2 million °C (3.6 million °F). Fountains of burning helium and hydrogen gas, called solar flares, shoot out from it into space.

Keeping warm

When you are asleep your body produces as much heat as a 100-watt lightbulb.

No people lived in North America until about 30,000 years ago. At that time, the sea levels were much lower, and hunters following herds could cross the Bering Strait on dry land from Asia.

Cockroach cure

About 2,000 years ago, a Greek doctor called Dioscorides Pedanius believed he had a cure for earache. All you had to do was scoop out a cockroach's stomach, mix it with oil, and stuff it in your ear. Later, another doctor said crushed cockroaches cured itching, swollen glands, and scabs. By the 1500s, cockroaches had spread all over the world and were a pest. Danish sailors earned a bottle of brandy if they killed 1,000 of them.

Guns into medals

Britain's highest military decoration for bravery is the Victoria Cross. Queen Victoria first awarded it in 1856, at the end of the Crimean War. For many years the crosses were made of bronze from Russian guns captured during the war.

More movies have been made featuring Sherlock Holmes than any other character in fiction. The famous detective, who always gets his man or woman, has been played by 68 actors in 187 movies.

Long story

Did you know that part of your food-processing system is a long tube called the small intestine, which is coiled up inside you? If you stretched it out, it would be 22 feet (6.7m) long. If you opened up all the tiny wrinkles in it, it would measure 360 sq yd (300.9 sq m).

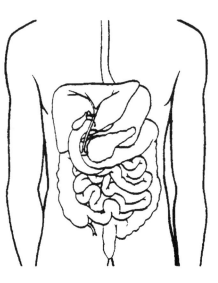

Whole new ball game

One of the world's most popular sports, so the story goes, was started by a British schoolboy. At Rugby School in 1823, William Webb Ellis was playing in a soccer game when he picked up the ball and ran with it. This was illegal, but it led to the start of a new ball game – rugby.

Seawater has a huge amount of salt dissolved in it. If all the salt could be taken out of the sea and spread over all the land in the world, it would cover the land with a layer of salt 500 feet (152.4m) thick.

Neck and neck

The longest neck of all, over 49 feet (14.9m) long, was that of the dinosaur Mamenchisaurus. It was over two-and-a-half times the height of a giraffe. Its neck had the same number of bones as a giraffe's neck.

Warrior queen

When the ancient Romans occupied Britain, Boudicca, the queen of an eastern tribe, rebelled. Her army attacked Roman towns and killed over 70,000 men, women, and children.

Every year, each person living in the United States uses things made from wood equal to one tree 100 feet (30.4m) tall. That comes to a forest of over 258 million trees in one year.

Cell-by date

The human body has about ten trillion cells. About three billion die every day and are replaced by new ones. The cells in your intestines last about three days, those in your liver about 18 months. Only the cells in your brain are never replaced.

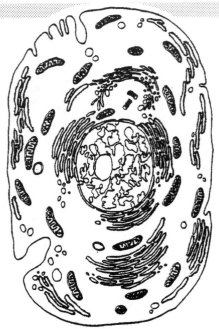

Light years away

Astronomers use the term "light years" to describe distances in space. There is a distant galaxy called 3C-295 which is 500 million light years away. What this really means is that it is 26,000,000,000,000,000,000,000,000 miles (41,800,000,000,000,000,000,000 km) away from Earth!

Hurricanes were first given names by Clement Wragge, an Australian weatherman. Known as "Wet Wragge," he used the names of people he had quarrels with for the worst storms.

Eye shadow

Ancient Egyptian women painted black eye makeup around their eyes. This helped to reduce the glare of the Sun.

Climbing crabs

Spider crabs live on islands in the Pacific and Indian oceans. They grow to be about 18 inches (45.7cm) long and have very long legs, which they use to climb trees. When a crab gets to the top of a tree, it snips off a young coconut with its huge pincers and climbs down again to eat it.

Giant midgets

This is the actual size of an ant. Those in hot, wet areas of the world can be more than 1 inch (2.5cm) long.

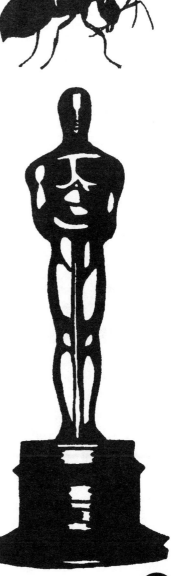

Uncle Oscar

Every year, the Academy of Motion Picture Arts and Sciences awards a trophy to people who have made an outstanding contribution to cinema. The trophy – a golden statue – used to be called The Statuette. In 1931, Margaret Herrick spotted a copy of it and said, "Why, he looks just like my uncle Oscar." Since then, the awards ceremony and the statuettes have been called Oscars.

Forming fingers and toes

For the first 40 days of a baby's growth within the womb, it has no fingers or toes – only flippers. The fingers separate around the 50th day, and the toes form a week later. The little black shape above is the actual size of a 40-day-old embryo.

Twinkle twinkle little star

Stars may look as bright as each other, but this can be misleading. The star Alnilan (**A**) is 26,000 times brighter than our Sun, while Bellatrix (**B**) is only 2,000 times brighter than our Sun. Both look smaller because Alnilan is more than three times farther away from Earth (**C**).

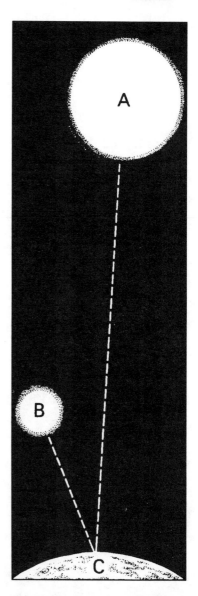

The great classical writers Homer, Horace, Virgil, and Plato all never saw a book. Books were only produced in the Western world after the years 1400–1500. Earlier writers read scrolls.

Customary death

Numbers of accidents in public places involving the custom of bowing are growing rapidly in Japan – 24 deaths have occurred in the last 5 years. At railways and airports many people have been knocked down escalators, nudged in front of trains, and trapped in revolving doors. Authorities are planning to install "greeting zones" in potentially hazardous areas.

Perpetual growth

All your body slows down its growth rate when you get older. Only your ears keep growing.

183

The American national anthem "The Star-Spangled Banner" was written in 1814 but only adopted over one hundred years later, in 1931.

Living dead

Seeds found in the tombs of ancient Egyptians when planted have blossomed into flowers. They have retained their life force for over 4,000 years.

Tail light

The Australians use camels to carry goods over dry barren land. When the camels journey down roads, to avoid accidents with vehicles approaching from the rear they have lights attached to their tails called "tail lights."

The Romans had no figure for zero. They used letters of the alphabet for the numbers 1, 5, 10, 50, 100, 500, and 1000. This meant that they couldn't add up in columns.

Playtime
William Shakespeare wrote *Romeo and Juliet* when he was 29 years old.

Mirror-writing Italian genius
Leonardo da Vinci was left-handed. In his notes and drawings of observations and ideas for inventions his writing goes from right to left and seems to be in a secret code. If you held his notebooks up in front of a mirror you could read them – if your Italian was good enough.

INDEX

189